Adventures in
Kate Bush
and Theory

Adventures in **Kate Bush** *and Theory*

Deborah M. Withers

HammerOn Press

Published by HammerOn Press 2010

ISBN 978-0-9564507-0-8

Adventures in Kate Bush and Theory / Deborah M. Withers
1. Bush, Kate - Criticism and interpretation. 2. Cultural studies - gender, sexuality and music.

First edition
2010
HammerOn Press, Bristol, UK
www.hammeronpress.net

Cover design by Caroline Duffy
www.carolineduffy.co.uk

Typeset by Michal William / Semi-Square
www.semi-square.co.uk
Set in Garamond and Myriad

dedicated to the fags

Adventures in Kate Bush and Theory would not have been possible without the support, love and inspiration from the following people:

Kris Hubley, Red Chidgey, Amy Lou Spencer, Molly James, Emma Thatcher, Edie Pain, May and John Withers, Paul Beswick, Ron Moy, Karren Ablaze, Caroline Duffy, Michal William/Cupid, Sal Harrington, Natalie J Brown, Dimitris Papadopoulos, Rose Clark, Lisa Brook, Melanie Maddison, Sophie Brown, Nicola Elliott and Sadie.

Thank you to Kate Bush, without whose music these thoughts would have never have happened.

Contents

Adventures in Kate Bush and Theory: Introduction

> [Kate Bush] supplies me with all the clues and it's up to me put the answers together – well that's the Koran of music – and that's surely what we're all looking for, no easy answers to anything.
>
> John Lydon[1]

Adventures in Kate Bush and Theory will present Kate Bush to you as you have never seen her before: the polymorphously perverse Kate, the witchy Kate, the queer Kate; the Kate who moves beyond the mime. To do this I need to tell a story, the story of the Bushian Feminine Subject (the BFS). The BFS is found within Bush's music but she is not the same as Bush herself. When Bush the person dies, the BFS will absolutely live on through her music. The BFS is a multiform character who appears across Bush's music and films and you will get to know her intimately. This book is the story of the BFS's movement through birth, performance, breakdown, death and rebirth. Finally it charts her disappearance into the landscapes of her own creation.

I call the book *Adventures in Kate Bush and Theory* to invite a sense of playfulness and wonder. These are two strategies which I think are important when engaging with Bush's work. The adventure emerges because her music provides an impressive terrain of codes and sources that can be deciphered given the appropriate tools. To put it another way; if Bush's music is a treasure map then the theory I use in this book are the clues in which to read it. What follows is the treasure. Within these pages I roam throughout her music, making connections and telling the stories that are embedded within them. For Bush is first and foremost a story-teller and invites a way of thinking and reading about her work that comes from this position.

When I combine 'Kate Bush' with 'Theory,' I want to build a creative theoretical narrative that tells a story. In the story, the BFS becomes a character who is, in many senses, independent of her creator. I want Bush's music to come alive in an experimental fashion but retain a focus on how it exists at the interrelation of popular culture, theory, art, the avant-garde, history and philosophy. I also want to demonstrate how sexuality, gender, power, race, class and spirituality shape her work. My desire is to move away from conventional uses of theory that are often found within academic writing. I want an adventure. These impulses shape this work because theory *can* be funny, sordid and relevant – despite what most people think. Theory can be used to tell and develop stories, and situate those stories within larger stories. These can help further understanding of the diverse political and social worlds we inhabit. Theory is useful to creative minds, as is Kate Bush.

Certain stories are always told about Bush in the popular media. The BBC's 2009 documentary, *Queens of British Pop*, contained many of them. It highlighted Bush's enigmatic nature, the uniqueness of her voice and her difference from the humdrum pop mainstream. She writes challenging songs which make the listener work to genuinely appreciate them. She was a pioneer of the music industry in the late 1970s where '"birds don't sell"'[2] and did not produce their own records. Ultimately fame was the 'unwanted consequence'[3] of her creative actions. The aim of this book is not to challenge these stories. They are the more flattering media myths that represent Bush within popular culture. We shouldn't forget the other myths that suggest she is a control-freak crazy recluse either.

While all of these myths contain shadows of truth within them, my aim is to engage with the myths that Bush created *within* her music. I am not interested in the popular mystery of the person but I *am* interested in creating further mysteries as I tell the life-story of the BFS, the multiform character who appears within Bush's music.

Part of the aim of this book is to situate the common, intuitive and everyday statements made about Bush within popular culture (for example, about the uniqueness of her voice) within philosophical writing. I will also explain how these ideas can also be linked to social and cultural change.

The beginning of the journey

Within this book I will focus on many of the albums and films that are neglected or easily dismissed when critics and commentators write about Bush. Again, there are often common stories that frame her creative output. *The Kick Inside* is the interesting debut which shows promise and the breakthrough hit, 'Wuthering Heights.' It is hastily followed by *Lionheart*, which is seen as a rushed affair and the result of industry pressure. *Never for Ever* is where Bush begins to gain control over the production of her music, as signs of her maturation as an artist emerge. *The Dreaming* is her 'crazy' album and receives polarised reviews (genius! or over-elaborate nonsense). *Hounds of Love* is considered her masterpiece. *The Sensual World* is said to be her 'female' album (as Bush herself described it). *The Red Shoes* is generally seen as an under-performer and its accompanying film, *The Line, the Cross and the Curve*, is basically erased from most critics' interest. After the much lamented twelve year absence from the public eye, *Aerial* is widely considered to be a return to form by critics and fans alike.

While these stories offer a way of framing understandings of Bush's music, they simply do not do justice to the complexity of albums such as *Lionheart*, *The Dreaming*, *The Red Shoes*, and films such as *The Line, the Cross and the Curve*. This complexity is the BFS. She (the BFS) moves through Bush's work and takes a different form in each release. Through getting to know the BFS, Bush's work will become more alive, unified and multiple. All too often *Hounds of Love* grabs the critical limelight and I want to engage with Bush's work that is pushed to the margins.

Much of the writing and media about Bush, certainly within popular culture, is produced or written by (now middle aged) heterosexual white men. They are either her contemporaries or enjoyed her music as a teenager. This is not to deny the validity or authority of such commentators to write about Bush's work. However what these men write often reproduces gendered and sexual cultural norms, purely by virtue of their frame of reference. My perspective is different. I am a white, queer woman in my late 20s and offer readings of Bush's work from a slightly different position. My perspective is sensitive to the marginalised, peculiar and downright weird voices within her music. These sing through the body of the BFS as she appears through Bush's career.

While subjectivity is the main focus of the book, I do not want to emphasise my own subjectivity too much. However, I will offer this disclaimer. Your experience, gender, sexuality, race, class, physical ability, age and so on matter in how you receive and interpret cultural messages. In other words, how I read Bush's music is going to be unique because my life experience creates a particular perspective from which I interpret Bush's music.

There are of course many interpretations of Bush's music that can be enjoyed by people interested in her work. They range from online blog entries to fan discussion forums[4] and magazines,[5] to music magazines to academic sources.[6] *Adventures in Kate Bush and Theory* is a small contribution to these unique responses to Bush's music.

I offer a queer feminist re-interpretation of Bush's music as told through the life of the BFS. This queered strategy (when queer is understood to query, question and disrupt) is reflected in the albums and films that I explore in the book. By focussing on Bush's neglected albums I hope to renew interest and appreciation of the highly engaging (as well as musically brilliant!) aspects of Bush's music.

How are we going to do this?

The main theoretical concept that is drawn upon within the book is *subjectivity.*[7] Subjectivity is what forms the 'life' of the BFS. At a very basic level, it should be understood as the 'I' that is found within, and as it moves through, Bush's music. These 'I's' (for they are multiple) undergo numerous changes over the range of albums that Bush has created in her career. I will chart their (non-linear) development as a journey that shifts between birth, death and rebirth.

These 'I's' are also subject to processes of negotiation *and* creativity. The negotiation of imposed identities (as derived from gender, race and class, for example), and the creativity it takes to produce new sites of gendered and sexual expression. These are not always 'known' in a pre-existent sense. They are made through unique acts of subject-making. These acts can be communicated through the body, but also, and importantly for an artist like Bush, through the singularity of her voice.

The BFS makes and negotiates her subjectivity in front of a large audience. Bush has sold millions of records and despite her reclusiveness remains a household name. The BFS creates more room for people to exist within their own subjectivities, 'room for life.'[8] She does this through the invention of characters and identities which often push the boundaries of gendered and sexual correctness. Likewise, the BFS equally reinforces conservative ideas about race and class. This emerges from Bush's own position as a white, middle class woman, the life experience which colours her perspective. These are important elements of subjectivity which the BFS traverses. They shape the ways she moves within (negotiates), remakes (transforms) and reinforces pre-existing patterns of the social world. She does so within popular music, which is her particular sphere of influence.

The BFS is simultaneously 'an active agent of social, political and cultural analysis and transformation'[9] as well as being 'outside itself, in the world of others, in a space and time it does not control.'[10] These are the two poles of negotiation and creativity that I referred to earlier.

Within the life of the BFS there is the body of a singing woman inserted into culture within particular moments in history. These moments will change throughout the book as she moves and grows against them. Within each moment a set of possibilities and options are open to her. These designate the boundaries in which she can express herself, claim social space, and assert her vocal uniqueness that sings itself to others.[11] She is cris-crossed in a theatre of power and culture which shapes her at least as much as she shapes it. In this way the BFS's approach to subjectivity is similar to a dialogue. She sings and moves against the structures and positions which are produced and imposed upon her. She also undoes and expands them with her actions.

Getting to know the BFS's voice and body

The singing body is an important site where these acts of dialogue occur. It is absolutely central to the BFS's remaking of the social world in the popular realm. The BFS is constituted by her always changing, acoustically sonorous and breathing body. In some cases bodily processes are the central, thematic inspiration points for the songs; *The Kick Inside* is an anthem to the creativity of female bodies. This bodily knowledge has been politically suppressed within western culture for, quite literally, millennia.[12] *The Kick Inside* contains a bodily resonance that is transmitted between bodies and ears who respond to it. However there is no uniform way of responding, and everyone experiences music in particular and unique ways. In other cases the body is enacted. There is singing not only with part of the body (the throat, for example) but with *the whole body*. Many of the vocal performances on *The Dreaming* are good examples of this. They lodge themselves into other bodies in acts of forceful transference.

I mention these points to foreground how the activities of the BFS actively disrupt the traditions of Western culture. Western culture has inherited a metaphysical tradition that carries an 'affinity for an abstract and bodiless universality.'[13] This creates the condition where the body is feared. Within music, this has certain implications. As Susan McClary writes:

> In many cultures, music and movement are inseparable activities, and the physical engagement of the musician in performance is desired and expected. By contrast, Western culture – with its puritanical, idealist suspicion of the body – has tried throughout much of its history to mask the fact that *actual people usually produce sounds* that constitute music. As far back as Plato, music's mysterious ability to inspire bodily motion has aroused consternation, and a very strong tradition in musical thought has been devoted to defining music as the sound itself, to *erasing the physicality involved in both the making and reception of music.* [14]

To understand the BFS, it is important to remember the physical or embodied quality of the music. This is apart from the actual body of Bush although it emerges from her. This embodied quality can have an impact on others who listen and are affected by it. It may be easy to think of music as ephemeral and without physical substance. However, to do this is to deny the way in which music creates the conditions where people can be responsive in an embodied manner.

An introductory map of the life of the BFS

Within this book you will embark on the journey of the BFS as she moves through Bush's music. You will move through desire, humour, pain and transformation, and gain some different perspectives on Bush's music along the way. Before we embark upon this journey, I will offer a brief outline of what to expect in each chapter. I will introduce you to the range of secondary guides who help me hold up the corners of the map.

Each chapter of this book will focus on a particular stage in the life of the BFS. I will apply or develop a theoretical framework to an album or collection of songs.

One: Emergence, *The Kick Inside*

On Bush's debut, *The Kick Inside,* the BFS is first invoked. Invocation highlights the importance of spirituality, witchcraft and the occult to the BFS's 'life.' The BFS has power to invoke 'strange phenomena' and explore the suppressed mysteries of the female body. On *The Kick Inside* the 'feminine' of the BFS is at its most forceful and recognisable. She draws upon the female body for creative inspiration, her rhythms, fluids and desire. I use feminist theories of the late 1970s that use the feminine and the female body as a site of difference, power and multiplicity to develop these ideas.

What happens on *The Kick Inside* is crucial for subsequent albums where the BFS forges her life path. Within the work there are a number of different thematic qualities or magickal[15] powers which are released within the thriving body of the work. These qualities are voice, fluidity, multiplicity, the body, desire, the irrational, taboo and rebirth. They will further understandings of the BFS in later albums. All of Bush's albums carry a mark of the BFS's initial, public invocation and *The Kick Inside* is an important reference point. It is the ground of being on which the BFS charts her creative journey.

Two: *Lionheart* and the Queer Life of the BFS

The BFS is a canny shape-shifter. On *Lionheart* she uses theatrical modes in which to explore, negotiate and create other subjectivities. Due to the theatrical backdrop and hyper-feminine, camp ambience which pervades the work, queer theories will be used to explore the play and negotiation of the BFS on *Lionheart. Lionheart* presents the BFS as a vanguard in relation to gender and sexuality. She freely explores transgendered identities and fantasises about gay male group sex. However, the BFS also perpetuates conservative ideas about Nationalism and Englishness. These deploy stereotypical motifs relating to western cultural imperialism, in particular Orientalism.

Never for Ever: the transition of the BFS

Between chapters two and three we will briefly visit some key moments from *Never for Ever*. This will help us ease the transition and further transformation of the BFS. *Never for Ever* will be presented as both looking back to her early incarnations, as well as looking forward to what will come on *The Dreaming*.

Three: Breakdown, *The Dreaming*

On the experimental work *The Dreaming*, a radical and traumatic breakdown happens in the life of the BFS. This breakdown is also a breakthrough into new understandings of relationships. These remake the BFS as her world is expanded through connections with machines and animals. The BFS's breakdown is partly a response to a growing awareness of the histories of exploitation, violence and colonialism in which she, as a white woman, is implicated. After her destruction comes a reconstruction, of herself and the social world she inhabits and reworks through her actions.

Four: Death, *The Red Shoes* and *The Line, the Cross and the Curve*

The Red Shoes and *The Line, the Cross and the Curve* effectively see the death of the BFS. It occurs as she attempts to negotiate her place in the fairy-tale, symbolic universe of 'The Red Shoes' story. This chapter is an example of the BFS 'in action' as she negotiates a story that radically pre-exists her.

For women, adorning the red shoes is a gesture that should never be entered into lightly. It results in a very gender specific death. This chapter will engage with previous uses of the red shoes in popular culture, such as Hans Christian Andersen's and Michael Powell and Emeric

Pressburger's versions of the story. Here the BFS will return to witchcraft and the occult in order to break the 'spell' of the red shoes story.

Five: The Rebirth ('The Ninth Wave') and Disappearance ('A Sky of Honey') of the BFS.

Within the life of the BFS, after death there will always be birth. This chapter uses the shamanic rebirth journey in 'The Ninth Wave' on *Hounds of Love* as a reference point to explore the concept of rebirth. Rebirth is central to the BFS's creative survival within Bush's music. As an idea, it allows us to see how the BFS moves between the boundaries of life and death and remakes herself continually.

Finally, the journey of the BFS ends with her disappearance on the 'Sky of Honey.' The 2005 album, *Arial*, signalled the literal rebirth of the BFS within Bush's music. While 'A Sky of Honey' mimics many of the patterns relating to rebirth within 'The Ninth Wave,' it is also crucially different. It relates to the rhythms of rebirth and emergence which exist within the natural world. The BFS disappears between bird song and the movement of light.

Within these five movements you will experience the non-linear journey of the BFS. She will experiment with form and technique, costumes and expression, desire and destruction. As secondary guides in this journey, I call upon a cast of critical thinkers to help us understand the BFS. These include the work of writers such as Hélène Cixous, Luce Irigaray, Gilles Deleuze and Felix Guattari, Adriana Cavarero, Donna Haraway, Starhawk and Rosi Braidotti. You will be presented with the avant-garde feminist theories of the 1970s (and their continued relevance), theories of difference, witchcraft, the goddess, queer and postcolonial theory, becoming, ethics, pain, trauma, post-humanism and the singularity and uniqueness of the voice.

Without further ado, we are now ready to commence the journey.

The Kick Inside: The Beginning of the Journey

We begin the journey of the Bushian Feminine Subject (BFS) by considering Kate Bush's debut album, *The Kick Inside. The Kick Inside* is important because it contains the seeds that enable the BFS to grow into different forms later in her life. Without such a beginning, the subsequent multiple qualities of the BFS would be substantially more difficult. One thing is certain in this story; the BFS never stays the same. My engagement with *The Kick Inside* explains how this is the case in her beginning.

Voice

Kate Bush is renowned for her unique and different voice. It is the first thing that most people notice about her. It is an assault on the normal parameters of vocal modulation. Voice too is one of the BFS's most powerful weapons. It is used to inhabit different characters and create multiple perspectives. She does this through contrasting uses of pitch, tone and utterance.

Within her life the BFS's voice moves between varieties of feminine subjectivities. These range from the girl, to the eunuch, to the deeper enunciations that are more suggestive of the emotionally mature woman. She 'croons lullabies, howls, gasps, babbles, shouts and sighs.'[1] It is the type of voice that Xavière Gauthier attributes to witches: '*Why witches*? Because witches sing.'[2] The BFS's voice is also non-linear. It shifts back and forth in time. It can be old when it is young, young when it is old and both of those things at the same time. It doesn't develop in a straightforward way. It refuses to 'speak straightforwardly, logically, geometrically, in strict conformity' with the prevailing rules of culture.[3]

The voice has a certain place (or more precisely, a lack of place) within the history of philosophy. This makes the weaponry of the BFS's voice even more significant and effective. Contemporary Italian philosopher Adriana Cavarero argues that hearing a voice 'communicates [...] precisely the true, vital, and perceptible uniqueness of the one who emits it.'[4] She asserts that recognising the uniqueness of voices enables listeners to gain an understanding of the human value of the person who is speaking. She describes this process as a 'duet, a calling and responding - or, better, a reciprocal intention to listen [...] that reveals and communicates everyone to the other.'[5] Cavarero's philosophy of the voice can be summarised as the recognition of unique voices. This highlights the listening relationship that is nurtured between ears and vibrating bodies. It is important for understanding the voice of the BFS.

Bush's voice is a forceful example of the process Cavarero describes. It is precisely the uniqueness of her voice that is immediately recognised by listeners. This happens often whether they like it or not (we do not choose to hear noise, it intrudes upon us). This potentially offers a vehicle for recognising the uniqueness of *all* voices. This is an important step that the cultural world would benefit from taking together. We cannot assume that all voices and all people are seen as unique or worth valuing. Some would argue that this is one of the greatest philosophical and political problems of all time. What is important is that the BFS creates a gateway for noticing the singular uniqueness of the voice which sings to others.

Her voice took people by surprise. At the time of her appearance the BFS's voice was quite literally 'unheard.' Nicky Losseff writes:

> Kate Bush's vocal quality – unknown to the public at the time of ['Wuthering Height's] release, and which would seem to have been the aspect of the song that struck the first-time listener most forcefully – transmits, at the juncture of language and pure sound, intuitive rather than cer-

> ebral meaning. Inside her voice, the listener participates in the essentially solipsistic world of the spirit.[6]

The voice of the BFS is also an indisputably female voice. Female voices within all realms of culture have a harder time being heard than male voices. This is true both throughout history and in contemporary times. Bush's early interviews indicate that she felt there was a lack of strong female voices from which she could gain inspiration in the 1970s.

> When I'm at a piano writing a song, I like to think I'm a man, not physically but in the areas that they explore. Rock 'n' Roll and punk, you know, they're both really male music, and I'm not sure I understand them yet, but I'm really trying. When I'm at the piano I hate to think that I'm a female because I automatically get a *preconception*. Every female you see at the piano is either Lynsey DePaul, Carole King... that lot. *And it's a very female style.*
>
> That sort of stuff is sweet and lyrical, but it doesn't push it on you, and most male music – not all of it, but the good stuff – really lays it on you. It's like an interrogation. It really puts you against the wall, and that's what I'd like to do. I'd like my music to intrude. It's got to.[7]

The 1970s saw an insurgence of women singer-songwriters, performers and bands. Artists like Patti Smith embraced androgyny and male rock ethics. Joni Mitchell wrote and produced successful albums on her own terms. Despite wide critical acclaim, both of these artists remained avant-garde figures, existing largely on the edges of the pop mainstream. The 1970s also saw a number of movements which challenged the gendered norms of the music industry. Glam rock glorified gender bending, theatricality and the cult of the pop star. Punk rock challenged notions of authority, mastery and genius which were endemic to rock as a genre. Punk in particular created a space where female musicians could pick up instruments and raise their voices.

Despite these emergent challenges to the male dominated music scene, Bush remained sceptical about the lack of female voices she could call upon as inspiration to support her own. For women it is always harder to speak if no other respected female artists have spoken before you. Famously, Bush called upon a guide from the previous century, Emily Brontë's Cathy, to help her make an impact within the pop charts.

Anyone who is savvy with Bush trivia will know that she didn't read *Wuthering Heights* before writing her number one hit. She only saw the last ten minutes of a TV adaptation which included a scene that was never in the original text. This doesn't really matter in terms of using Brontë as a foremother. The symbolic resonance of the title remains. It invokes the power of allusion.

'Wuthering Heights' introduced the public not necessarily to Kate Bush the singer, but to a character who is representing a ghost. 'I really try to project myself into the role of Cathy and so, as she is a ghost, I gave her a high-pitched wailing voice.'[8] Cathy is given the central voice and speaks through the BFS. She uses her body and voice as a vessel for the expression of a spirit that is refusing to leave the mortal world and its inhabitants in peace.

Female voices haunt the dominant social reality by not appearing fully present in the way that men's voices do. Stereotypically, men's deeper pitched voices communicate authority and power. Women's voices are often higher, and are not taken seriously in the same way.[9] There is no attempt in 'Wuthering Heights' to gain access to a 'fully present' female voice. It embraces the position that the female voice *is* a ghost. The song refuses assimilation into the fully present conception of the female voice. The experience is culturally haunting. Can women assert their voices without compromise within a male-defined cultural sphere? What suggestions do female artists need to make to define their voice on their own terms? Such a suggestion is found in 'Wuthering Heights.' The song makes an absent female voice overwhelmingly powerful; 'The absence of a Witch does not/ Invalidate the Spell –.'[10]

The lyrics of 'Wuthering Heights' express the desires of an obsessive, brooding and determined spirit. 'Too long I roam in the night/ I'm coming back to his side to put it right.'[11] The final refrain of 'Oh let me have it, let me grab your soul away' (*KI*), underlines the intention of the spirit to inhabit a realm unjustly taken away from her. The song's persistence rectifies the injustice of this premature death and the silence this entails. The persistence of returning is a marked quality of the BFS's life.

The problem of highlighting the female voice's silence throughout history and culture is achieved by asserting its absence. It is in this paradoxical space that the BFS finds herself. Silent and absent while being present and effective. As a public introduction, such a performance demands a shift which transforms common cultural listening practices. It allows the BFS's challenging voice to be heard on its own terms. It refuses assimilation and affirms its uniqueness, its difference. This difference is then recognised by others.

French philosopher Luce Irigaray describes such a transition as entering into the culture of breath: 'Listening to the spirit instead of the letter,' she argues, could bring forth the 'recognition of feminine qualities.' Here 'the time of spirit could be the time of a culture of the breath [...] that could be shared by men and women beyond the particularities of their languages and systems of representations.'[12]

Listening to the spirit - in this case the literal ghost Cathy represents - provides an avenue to the recognition of the feminine and the uniqueness of female voices. The BFS makes it easy for listeners to connect with the spirit by presenting her voice as a ghost. When the BFS performs Cathy, even the most obstinate listener is forced into communion with her voice.

Voice is a central tool that the BFS will use in her life.

Fluidity

One of the main qualities of the BFS is her fluidity. She challenges the idea that identities are linear. The BFS does not progress, she shifts backwards and forwards. She is susceptible to influence. She changes shape. The BFS does not see identity as a closed question. Fluidity is about movement between categories. The BFS's fluidity allows her to inhabit a spectrum of identities. It also designates a freer state of movement - of body, imagination and desire. This is also connected to the different bodily rhythms of women. Fluidity can also literally refer to the variety of women's bodily fluids that are celebrated on this album.

Fluidity is about how the songs on the album relate to each other. Many of the songs on *The Kick Inside* are subject to a fairly traditional verse/chorus song structure. However the continuity between the songs creates the feeling of a journey. This undermines traditional song structures as they segue into one other. The effect is circular: refusing closure and a definite end.

The Kick Inside opens with 'Moving.' This immediately introduces a space of fluidity through its lyrics. 'Moving' presents an endearing and simple invitation addressed to a listening stranger. The song suggests this stranger can experience new desires and access exciting dimensions as long as s/he can feel the movement. The opening, punctuated by whale noises, offers the seductive statement: 'Moving stranger, does it really matter?/ As long as you're not afraid to feel' (*KI*). This beckons the listeners to come closer to the BFS.

The BFS asks the listening stranger to abandon sceptical preconceptions and intellectual understandings. Instead they must draw upon feelings. The BFS's 'open arms ache' (*KI*) with anticipation. Movement is grounded in generative desire: 'How I'm moved, how you move me/ With your beauty's potency/ You give me life, please don't let me go' (*KI*). The life-giving ability of the listener is here emphasised. S/he is given an active role in helping to create the life energy of the BFS. This point resonates with Cavarero's conception that the speaking or singing voice is always speaking *to* another voice. We are formed within that relation.

'Moving' becomes a space in which to build and experience this relation. From the first lyrical strains of the album, listeners are encouraged to participate and enter into a relationship of mutual renewal. This point about relationality is similar to Irigaray's conclusion from her research into linguistics. She concluded that 'the difference between the sexes was above all a relational identity.'[13]

Irigaray's ideas about sexual difference are complex. She has often been criticised for her argument that a fundamental sexual difference exists between men and women. The critique lies in the assumption that this argument promotes an essential, biological difference between men and women. However, as the above quote suggests, this difference is relational, not biological. It cannot be reduced to bodies. It resides more in how we are positioned to each other. It is this kind of relational knowledge that the BFS embodies on 'Moving.' Importantly, it is a relational knowledge that any person, with any kind of body, can participate in. Sexual difference does not divide men and women, nor does it exactly bring them together. Rather, it highlights different ways of relating with and to each other.

The second verse of 'Moving' articulates fluid tendencies more directly: 'Moving liquid, yes, you are just as water/ You flow all around that comes your way' (*KI*). This statement confers upon listeners a liquid state of being. While the process 'sets your spirit dancing' (*KI*), creating awareness of energy flows, suggesting there is a bodily energy connected to the spirit. There is impulse to abandon the thinking self and submit to bodily possession. This flows into the spirit of the song. Flowing with others, merging with the world, the BFS is characterised by permeable ego boundaries. It is a state of receptivity, instinctively, creatively, emotionally and spiritually. This leads to a positive dissolution of the ego. This willingness to submit to this fluid process is again similar to Irigaray. Compare the lyrics of 'Moving' to Irigaray's inscription of the difference of the female subject:

> You are moving. You never stay still. You never stay. You never 'are.' How can I say 'you,' when you are always the other? How can I speak to you? You remain in flux, never congealing or solidifying. What will make that current flow into words? It is multiple, devoid of causes, meanings, simple qualities. Yet it cannot be decomposed. These

> movements cannot be described as the passage from beginning to end. These rivers flow into no single, definitive sea. These streams are without fixed banks, this body without fixed boundaries. This unceasing mobility.[14]

The two passages are extremely similar in the way they describe fluidity. They encompass the effect on the body, consciousness and movement. Transforming, shifting, powerful. Irigaray's statement suggests there is a kind of violence in the act of trying to pin down a person or identity that is always moving. It questions acts of naming – 'how can I say "you"?' It instils there a moment of doubt. This opens a space to question the fixing of identities within enclosed spaces: man/woman, gay/straight, to name the familiar and obvious few. What the BFS and Irigaray encourage is a stutter. This stutter suspends the fixity that occurs when people are named (or name themselves) as one thing or another. Instead, they both present a terrain of fluid positions which a person can move between as and when they want or need to.

The BFS is positioned in a fluid manner. She has permeable ego boundaries and is capable of merging with other subjects to create new subjectivities. Her fluidity means she is free to move away from restrictive or pre-conceived structures of movement and desire. This ability to move will serve her well in later years. She will pass easily into terrains of possibility that have no definite end. With her she carries the promise of transformation and movement.

Multiplicity

The BFS is made up of multiple subjectivities. She is programmed to proliferate and change. She is able to imagine herself outside culturally sanctioned limits. She can stretch and move these boundaries in many directions within her immediate spheres of knowledge and influence. The BFS's multiplicity arises from her ability to inhabit new and pre-existing characters. She resurrects stories and myths. 'Wuthering Heights' is an example of this, as is 'The Kick Inside,' which we will consider later.

Storytelling enables the BFS to occupy multiple positions. She never speaks as a single, identifiable 'I.' She creates a wider imaginative arena, encompassing a multitude of characters. This is the crux of her possibility. While this can be said to be true for many songwriters who tell stories, the difference with the BFS is how she generates difference through her multiplicity. Multiplicity is a strategy through which she claims power for herself and for others.

Often with singer songwriters there is the idea that 'the popular song serves as a form of personal confession.'[15] That is, the song will reveal an authentic or intimate 'truth' from the singer's soul or experience. Using popular song in this manner radically curtails the spaces the song can create. It also establishes narrow and distinct boundaries between the speaking subject and the 'listener' rather than opening it up. The BFS uses the popular song to explore multiple sites of speech, style, movement and action. This creates an elasticity of positions. This opens up space for new articulations of desire. These had been limited for women performers within popular music before the *The Kick Inside* was released in 1978.

An example of this inhabitation of characters is 'James and the Cold Gun.' The song tells the story of James, a cowboy outlaw who is 'running away from humanity' (*KI*). In 'James and the Cold Gun,' listeners are transported to the raw world of boy gangs swigging on whiskey, gamblers, pursuit, a whore 'still a-waiting in her big brass bed' (*KI*) and the renegade figure of James. The rawness of this outlaw world is communicated via the energetic vocal performance and the throbbing, excited thrusts of echoing electric guitars. The song's heavy rock posturing is in contrast to most of the other songs on the album. This contributes to the multiple fabrics of sound and rhythm that the work contains. These fuel the multiple qualities of the BFS.

'James and the Cold Gun' is a camp prog-rock parody, containing all the dramatics of prog, neatly contained within a 3 minute pop song. It sends up the stereotypical masculinity of the genre whilst demonstrating a divergence from conventionally 'feminine' styles of song writing. Humour is important and can be felt in the 'coldness' of James' gun (usually cowboys are 'hot shots'). The BFS does masculinity with charm, melodrama and hyperbole. The BFS does not restrict herself to conventionally gendered genres. She is able to move between gendered spaces with humour and ease.

Using a form of male rock style allows the BFS greater freedom of movement within the arena of the song. Although there seems to be little gender ambiguity when listening to the distinctively high-pitched, female and virtually hyper-feminine voice, this can be deceptive. The BFS crosses a range of gendered positions in her performance. In doing so she queers or feminises masculinity and masculinises femininity. She radically opens up gendered space to multiple possibilities.

Multiplicity also emerges from the embodiment of female sexuality that is explored on *The Kick Inside*. The free expression of female sexuality should not be taken for granted. It was (and arguably remains) a suppressed site of bodily knowledge that harbours revolutionary potential. Irigaray comments: 'We haven't been taught, or allowed, to express multiplicity. To do that is to speak improperly.'[16] To do so is to challenge the sexual boundaries of culture which have too often remained static.

French feminist writing of the late 70s stated freely that a woman's sexuality is multiple. It emphasised the heightened eroticism of the female body, which is reflective of the multiple sex organs that women have. These can be found in clitoris, breasts, anus and cunt. As Irigaray has commented, 'the plurality of the female orgasm...focuses on the multiple and heterogeneous pleasures located in the female body.'[17] This body has been denied its multiplicity, multi-vocity and presence within culture.

This multiple body is the body of the BFS. Her passion, fluidity and excess are propelled into motion on *The Kick Inside*. The album contains numerous instances of the simmering physicality of the female sexual body, while the vocal performance highlights its bodily production. This female body is a de-essentialised body. It draws upon the body but is not reduced to it. The BFS is not frightened of using her flesh as a source of inspiration and power.

Multiplicity as a starting point is important as it enables further differences to emerge. Multiplicity in the case of the BFS emerges partially from celebrating the embodied sexuality of the female body. Once the conditions for the multiplicity have been created, this energy can go anywhere and take on any form. It does not have to stay within a female body. It does not belong to it. Multiplicity can't be owned. Multiplicity connects. The female body is one vehicle among many.

Recognising sexual difference is part of Irigaray's philosophical project that I have been referring to in this book. Sexual difference is not the same as recognising that 'Men are from Mars and Women are from Venus.' This happens in popular culture all the time. Rather it is saying that there are different ways of being which need to be integrated into culture. This must change the ground of being rather than being assimilated or appropriated. To recognise something is for society to *really* change, for it to be different. This difference is bodily, sexual and relational. It is rhythmic, fluid, social and political; just like the BFS.

Another key to the BFS's multiplicity is her use of voice. This enables her to create a number of perspectives in a song. For example, 'Them Heavy People' is a personal song about learning from inspiring mentors. The BFS uses her voices in order to create multiple layers and dimensions of subjectivity. These transform the song from a confession of singular experience to a celebratory, multi-vocal event. As the song begins, the phrase 'Rolling the Ball' is repeated. This is echoed by layers of voices which are placed behind the central vocal line. This motif is repeated throughout the song. As a result, the idea that there is a central or singular subjectivity is displaced into a multiplicity of articulations. The use of the BFS's voice in this manner is a technique that is explored to a greater degree in her later albums, but begins on *The Kick Inside*.

The BFS accesses multiplicity in a number of ways: Through her play of gender in songs like 'James and the Cold Gun,' her consistent embodiment of multiple feminine subjectivity, her use of many different voices in the songs, and through her penchant for theatricality.

The Body

The BFS has a body that can move and move structures. The physicality of *The Kick Inside* communicates a desiring female body to popular culture. Listeners are encouraged to 'feel the music.' Songs draw their subject matter from women's bodily experiences, in particular childbirth and menstruation. It is important to draw attention to the bodily aspect of the BFS. It is this that will contort, fragment, merge and undergo a number of powerful transformations within this book.

Highlighting the body of the BFS is important because the female body is traditionally objectified within Western cultural representations. Often women have systematically been denied the active role of articulating their own bodily resonances. Over time the female body has been subject to a number of negative figurations. These reinforce the cultural idea that the female body needs to be contained or 'cured' of its volatile impulses.[18] These two factors combined have alienated and demonised the female body within culture. They have served to deny, censor and outline the limits of the female subject's self-representation and articulation of her own body.

Bodies have enormous potential to produce many different kinds of rhythms through musical expression. Music, in turn, is 'unignorably relational: it emanates, propagates, communicates, vibrates, and agitates; it leaves a body and enters others; it binds and unhinges, harmonises and traumatizes; it sends the body moving, the mind dreaming, the air oscillating.'[19] Receiving and producing music, sound and vibrations is thus a social and potentially powerful, connective experience.

Western culture has a habit of censoring certain kinds of bodies (women's bodies, queer bodies, dis/abled bodies, multi-racial bodies) and the alternative perspectives they draw attention to. It also privileges the mind over the body. This valorises rational thinking and the importance of the mind. It also relegates the body's importance and denies the value of feelings or emotions. Within traditional philosophical discourses, 'the body has been regarded as a source of interference in, and a danger to, the operations of reason.'[20] Through her body the BFS stresses the importance of feeling, emotion and sensation. She rejects the rationalism of the mind/body split. She oozes with sexuality and liquid.

The body of the BFS on *The Kick Inside* is striking for its power and autonomy. It is an ideal body. It is erotic, supple and articulate. It will not stay the same throughout her life. It is subject to various transformations. Such statements imply that the BFS is free to move in the world where and how she wants to. She is a fiction, so why shouldn't she be free? As much as she creates a space to be heard she also has to negotiate restrictions that are imposed upon her. The BFS is engaged in a bodily struggle against systems of co-option and restraint.

Desire

The BFS is an autonomously desiring and autoerotic subject. This means she doesn't 'need' anyone to satisfy her sexually because she can satisfy herself. Her sexuality is active. She foregrounds her physicality and the importance of sensation. She celebrates her ability to 'feel.' The turn to feeling activates emotion as a positive force. This is normally denied in a culture that values reason and rationality over emotional understanding.

Women have often been placed as objects, not subjects of desire. In this light, the active sexuality of the BFS is even more significant. Her desire is not merely directed toward a masculine object, it is directed toward herself. The BFS's desire enables her future expressions. It also creates a terrain of active spaces for other women to act from. By claiming a position of active desire, the BFS 'escapes' from the structural position of passivity women are socialised to occupy within patriarchal cultures.

Desire can be communicated through a number of avenues. Elizabeth Wood, a queer music theorist, locates desire in what she calls the 'Sapphonic Voice.' This voice has exceptional range and flexibility. It has the power to 'cross...boundaries among different voice types and their representations to challenge polarities of both gender and sexuality as these are socially and vocally constructed.'[21] This is the voice of the BFS. Wood goes on to argue that:

> the Sapphonic voice is a destabilizing agent of fantasy and desire. The woman with this voice, this capacity to embody and traverse a range of sonic possibilities and overflow sonic boundaries, may vocalize inadmissible sexualities and a thrilling willingness to move beyond the so-called natural limits, an erotics of risk and defiance, *a desire for desire itself.*[22]

The BFS's voice moves 'beyond the natural limits.' It shatters boundaries and contained sites of desire. It is destabilizing and it demands to be heard. It displays a desire for desire itself. Although self-sustaining, it may generate an awareness of other 'inadmissible sexualities'. It transfers desire infectiously. Although masturbatory, this desire does not belong only to the BFS. It is a desire useful to others who hear that voice. Through hearing it, they too may be awakened into the possibilities of autonomous desire.

The BFS is autoerotic because the female body and experiences form the subject-matter of her songs. 'Kite' and 'Room for Life' describe the bodily and cultural experiences of women in a way that is independent of male-defined narratives. This produces a femio-centric mythology of the body. They are inspired by female experience, and emerge from an engagement with the different rhythms of the female body. This produces a specifically female-identified desire which can be directed toward men or women.

This may seem to be suggesting there is some kind essential truth of the female body. Feminists have seen this as a risky strategy to engage with because throughout the ages women have been defined and confined by their biology. The ability to carry children in their bodies or their unpredictable hormones meant that the woman's rightful place is in the home as mothers or in the mental asylum. 'Biology is not destiny!' is an important slogan from the Women's Liberation Movement. However, *The Kick Inside* presents the female body in a powerful, creative and lasting way. The BFS draws upon the body as a creative source but is not reduced to it. Body and desire are linked.

Contemporary male reviewers detected the power of the BFS. They drew attention to the fact that *The Kick Inside* is an album saturated with sex and sexuality:

> A lot of people are not going to like what they hear Kate Bush saying in her new album THE KICK INSIDE, about being a woman in the seventies. And perhaps even more are going to object to the way that she says it, for in many of her songs she treads on a territory (sex as sex as sex) long held to be a male preserve.[23]

The defensive tone of the reviewer, Peter Reilly, creates an impression of the impact of the album upon contemporary listeners. It shows how the BFS's desire charted new territories for women's music and sexuality. The BFS was shocking. Reilly clearly suggests that what is challenging about the BFS is that she ventures into male cultural preserves – mainly the territory of active desire and sexuality. She is a 'woman of the seventies,' because she reflects the climate of emancipation of that time. The direct quality of the BFS is referred to in the statement 'the way that she says it.' Here he is referring to a sexuality that is grounded in the female body, its vibrations and sensations.

With the BFS, sex and desire are very much connected to pleasure. Sex as sex as sex, as Reilly would say, independent of its reproductive function. The sexual acts of the BFS can also seem free from power relations and hierarchy. There is a fusion of compatible and willing bodies and elements. Consider the lyrics and rhythms of the song 'Feel It,' a sultry piano-led meditation on the glory of sexuality: 'Nobody else can share this/ Here comes one and one makes one/ The glorious union, well, it could be love/ Or it could be just lust, but it will be fun/ It will be wonderful' (*KI*).

The first line of this verse creates a moment of intense intimacy between the BFS and her imagined lover, 'nobody else can share this.' 'The glorious union' is a phrase often used to describe the marital state. Here it is placed in the context of the speculative non-commitment of a casual sexual encounter. The playful and ambivalent 'It could be love/ or it could be just lust,' is overshadowed by the assertion and certainty that it 'will be fun' and 'it will be wonderful' (*KI*). Here, enjoyment alone is the key factor.

The chorus of the song instructs both listener and lover (the listener as lover) to 'Feel It.' This is repeated eight times, interspersed with orgasmic 'ohs,' while it changes halfway to 'Oh, I need it' (*KI*). The intensity is built throughout the chorus as the body presses deeper upon the piano to the final climax of 'Feel it! See what you're doing to me' (*KI*). This moves into a more gentle reflective tone, before the situation is continued in the second verse. Again there is a privileging of feelings and sensation over a rational thinking self. The second verse continues in a similarly explicit manner: 'Feel your warm hand walking around/ I won't pull away, my passion always wins/ So keep on a-moving in, keep on-a tuning in/ Synchronise rhythm now' (*KI*).

The line 'Feel your warm hand walking around' is teasingly descriptive and explicit. It presents a person familiar with being touched intimately. The next line - 'my passion always wins' - is the force that propels the life of the BFS. It is this desire or 'passion' that infuses her with life; it 'always' wins and thus influences her actions. The final couplet of the song returns to the idea of consensual union, embodied in a synchronicity of desiring and bodily rhythms, figured in explicit poetic language describing the execution of a sexual event. Again this charts a different configuration of desire based upon mutuality. It invokes and enacts a more egalitarian sexual relation between women and men.

Irigaray has written of the multi-sensational nature of women's bodies, and the ability to access sexual sensation in a number of different places:

> Fondling the breasts, spreading the lips, stroking the posterior wall of the vagina, brushing against the mouth of the

> uterus... pleasure(s) which are somewhat misunderstood in sexual difference as it is imagined – or not imagined, the other sex being the only indispensable complement to the only sex. But woman has sex organs more or less everywhere. *She finds pleasure almost everywhere.*[24]

The multiple sexual body that Irigaray describes resonates within the BFS: 'I'm dying for you just to touch me/ And feel all the energy rushing right up-a-me' (*KI*). The energy and desire invoked by the body, and an infatuated imagination in the throes of heady romance, are also found in the song 'L'Amour looks something like you': 'The thoughts of you sends me shivery/ I'm dressed in lace sailing down a black reverie/ My heart is thrown to the pebbles/ And the boatmen' (*KI*).

Here romance takes on a poetic form. The presence of water, motion and a lack of control are suggested by the sailing in 'reverie' of a heart that is 'thrown.' Here the body, romance and the imagination are entwined in the shivering body of the speaker. While the imagery of this song is less explicit than that of 'Feel It,' there is still the portrayal of a hedonistic sexual encounter emerging from drunken revelry: 'All in order, we move into the boudoir/ But too soon, the morning has resumed' (*KI*). In song structure, 'L'Amour' complements 'Feel It' in the sense that the chorus contains a concluding climax that trails off before re-entering in the second verse. While differently paced - 'Feel It,' being slow and sultry, and 'L'Amour' more of an upbeat pop song - they both attempt to create a climax within the song.

It is hugely important that this song doesn't describe a gender-specific sexual affair. This is the same with a number of the songs on the album: 'Oh to be in Love,' 'Feel It,' and 'Moving.' Other songs dramatise the female body ('Kite') and experience ('Room for the Life') so that desire is firmly situated within the feminine. Obviously some songs are addressed to men – 'Saxophone Song,' 'The Man with the Child in His Eyes' and 'Wuthering Heights.' They are never in the tradition of songs that reiterate the traditional relationship between women and men. They disrupt stereotypical narratives of desire. For example a woman objectifies a male saxophonist, the dramatisation of father-daughter relationship or by reinterpreting a literary narrative and mobilising it to articulate an absent female voice.

The absence of a gender-specific address creates multiple spaces of desired identification for the listener. It creates space for fantasy and exploration. Desire is more than which is contained by compulsory heterosexuality.[25] For the BFS, it means that she can sing and express desire independently of hetero-patriarchal cultural narratives. She can create them anew, free from pre-existing restrictions. It is a simple technique to experiment with, but by merely freeing desire from a situation where pronouns – such as 'he' and 'she' – do not matter or exist; it places no gendered limitations on the listener or the BFS. It also opens up space for the emergence of new configurations of desire.

The BFS draws upon the female body as a site in which to generate her auto-erotic desire. She displays a flagrant attitude of desire for the sake of desire. She engages in mutual, synchronised love-making. She removes cultural markers such as 'he' and 'she,' thus opening up desire to a terrain of identification unrestricted by gender.

The Irrational

The BFS celebrates the supposedly irrational aspect of women's lives, their volatile unpredictable bodies. She connects this to supernatural and unknowable phenomena. These help her celebrate female-centred forms of divinity.

The BFS invokes the power of the Goddess. She did this at a time in the late 1970s when these forms of knowledge and practices were being revitalised and discussed.[26] As Carol P. Christ has written, 'One of the most unexpected developments of the late twentieth century is the rebirth of the religion of the Goddess in western cultures.'[27] The Goddess is important, Christ argues, because it 'calls us to transform powerful, pervasive, and long-lasting images and ideas about God. We have been taught that God is male, that he transcends the earth and the body.'[28]

Goddess-based spirituality is immanent spirituality. It is connected to divinity of *this* world – for example to divinity of the earth, trees and rivers. It locates the divine within humans and animals. That means that God(dess) is everywhere, heaven is a place on earth and going to the woods is the same as going to Church. As a value system it provides an alternative to the hierarchies and dualisms that are at the core of Western culture's belief systems. Traditionally they privilege transcendence, detachment, objectivity and a belief in the rational self.[29] On *The Kick Inside*, the BFS offers a counterpoint to this system. She celebrates the irrational in her songs, aligning her music with the recovery of female-centred images, mythologies and rhythms.

The BFS celebrates the female body as divine flesh. Irigaray suggests that an acceptance of the feminine divine is vital for the recognition of equality between the sexes. She argues that 'women lack a female god who can open up the perspective in which *their* flesh can be transfigured.'[30] Her theory of sexual difference encompasses an understanding of spirit as well as bodies and relationality.

The so-called 'madness' and excessiveness of female experience is a continual source of inspiration for the BFS. These expressions of female 'madness' are celebrated from the onset of the BFS's life. They affirm such behaviour within popular culture where she charts her influence. It was a lot easier for women to be mad, bad and dangerous to know after the BFS. The 'irrational' should be understood in a positive sense for the BFS. Freed from a connection with the pathological, it is communicated through songs that celebrate supernatural occurrences and the subject of menstruation.

Menstruation remains a taboo topic within culture. It has consistently been associated with fear and dread. As Marie Mulvey-Roberts suggests,

> menstrual taboo is a complex and contested concept that has been protective and oppressive to women. Within mythology, literature and history, it has been displaced onto images that invoke holy dread, horror and awe such as the medusa, the vampire and female stigmatic.[31]

Instead, the BFS offers an embodiment of menstrual energy that is affirmative and creative. Her contribution to menstrual mythologies moves away from polarised representations such as Mulvey-Roberts describes.

There are two songs in particular on *The Kick Inside* that celebrate the irrationality of the BFS. They approach menstruation not as a disease that can be cured, contained and controlled, but rather as a type of magical power. This power is available for women to tap into. It is specifically theirs. All of *The Kick Inside* is arguably 'menstrual-driven.' However, 'Strange Phenomena' and 'Kite' are placed together in a way that suggests their mutual and compatible nature. Many of the songs that share similar themes are like this. 'Strange Phenomena' opens with an anticipatory, lingering and sinister piano riff that repeats and circles upon itself. Topically, menstruation is linked with the moon, the paranormal and inexplicable forces of creativity. The decision to combine the subject matter in this way invests menstrual power with a force which is both super-rational and supernatural. It also revitalises the cultural link between women's bodies and the tides of the moon: 'Soon it will be the phase of the moon/ When people tune in/ Every girl knows about the punctual blues/ But who's to know the power/ Behind our moves?' (*KI*).

Linking menstruation to the paranormal highlights the unknown quantity of menstrual energy. It affirms its relation to the imagination and creativity. The song suggests it is a blank, undefined space that can be opened up and explored. It is yet to be realised, but certainly not to be feared or suppressed. The 'punctual blues' is a neat synonym for Pre-Menstrual Tension. Instead of it being a medical condition, it is presented as a creative tool only available to girls. This song also echoes the argument of Penelope Shuttle and Peter Redgrove's book, *The Wise Wound*. It provided, in the late 1970s, a similar counter-cultural argument:

> menstruation is a great and neglected resource. It is also an evolutionary force. In modern times, it has not only been

> neglected, it has operated as a persecution, in which women are treated as inferior, because they bleed monthly, and, apparently, uselessly. Thus neglected, menstruation has turned into a sickness. Its language has been pain and sorrow.[32]

By linking the process of menstruation to creativity, the song moves away from the idea that women bleed uselessly. It suggests that there is more to menstruation than giving women the biological capacity to give birth. The chorus is an anthem to the 'strange' forces emanating from women's bodies: 'Raise our hands to the strange phenomena' (*KI*). The seeming peculiarity of women's seeping bodies is granted a positive figuration, in all of their beautiful strangeness. The song is an anthem to the irrational with its combination of paranormal beliefs, the power of synchronicity and changeable moods. 'Strange Phenomena' also contains the Buddhist chant 'Om mani padme hume.' This appears as a repeated mantra as the song runs into 'Kite.' The phrase roughly translates as 'Behold! The jewel in the lotus!' The 'jewel' that is sung of is the lily, which:

> with its showy blooms and yoni-shaped seed cases, is an ancient symbol of the female, both earthly and divine. Lilies press their way up through the soil to alert the world that spring is beginning and the growing, greening days of the Goddess have begun.[33]

Lily imagery also appears on 'Moving.' The BFS sings 'You crush the lily in my soul' (*KI*). The BFS draws upon the energy and existence of female-centred goddess imagery in order revitalise counter-female mythologies. These spiritual hymns to the goddess and the feminine can be found throughout the BFS's life. Later I will explain how they are a central part of understanding her movement in the world, in particular within her interpretation of 'The Red Shoes.'

While 'Strange Phenomena' celebrates women's menstrual capacities in its subject matter, 'Kite' *enacts* these menstrual rhythms. The image of 'Kite,' or becoming a kite, is one of the most important for the album.

Not only is it one of the most warped and idiosyncratic songs on the album (originally conceived as a type of Bob Marley reggae song), the image on the cover of *The Kick Inside* is of Bush with a kite attached to her back. On 'Kite' we find an example of menstrual rhythms. There is also a kind of 'menstrual muse.' This is another example of the autoeroticism that makes up the BFS: 'Beelzebub is aching in my belly-o/ My feet are heavy and I'm rooted in my wellios' (*KI*).

Menstrual energy is figured as a site of wonder, creativity, pleasure and pain. The BFS is prompted to become a kite flying on the wind. There is a strange irrational clarity to the song with its humour, excitement and bouncing movement. The chorus mimics the action of the kite's diving, flying and soaring. The song suggests that there is immense pleasure to be found listening to personal bodily rhythms and letting go. It charts an imagined flight through the air. The song recommends that listeners do not resist this motion, but rather respond intuitively through the body. In this way it does not place so much emphasis on the mind. Indeed the whole album is the product of a body affecting the mind and a mind listening to its body: 'Only look, trust the bleeding.'[34]

The ecstasy of becoming a kite is conveyed in the chorus: 'Come up and be a kite/ And fly a diamond night' (*KI*), and later 'Over the lights, and under the moon/ Over the lights, under the moon/ Over the moon, over the moon (*KI*). The childlike repetition of words and phrases, as well as the invocation of moon power, convey a sense of menstrual energy and wonder.

The character that becomes a kite, that rises and flies up and over the moon, is similar to a witch. The kite is a broomstick; 'What is a witch? A witch is a woman with strange powers... She rides to Sabbath on a broomstick... She worships the goddess of the moon, she operates in covens of thirteen persons... she is concerned with turning ordinary ideas upside down.'[35] On *The Kick Inside* the BFS is concerned with turning ordinary ideas upside down. The album also has thirteen songs on it. As Gauthier states: 'Why witches? *Because witches dance...* Why witches? *Because witches sing*.'[36] Images of witches, witchcraft and the occult are an important part of BFS's mythologies. They will be explored in depth later on in the book. These powers are first invoked on *The Kick Inside*. They are an important part of the BFS's immanent force and power.

The enduring image in 'Kite' of a human flying, swooping on, with and through the wind, also communicates the idea of the mind in imaginative flight. Importantly, this is prompted by the devil 'aching' in the belly of the BFS. Between these two songs, a space is created where the irrational rhythms, experiences and fluids of women's bodies are used in a creative moment. These can be treated directly as subject matter, or communicated via a rhythmical structure, as in 'Kite.' A new language of menstrual expression is being created.

The BFS forces the female body, with its different rhythms and fluid cyclical movement, into a culturally intelligible form that can be heard, felt and danced to. It offers the opportunity to relearn what is denied to women in terms of rhythm, myth, energy and power. It provides an embodied space of rhythm and infectious celebration. It offers the promise of the magic of menstruation and of listening to the body. It shows the potential that the irrational can be venerated, legitimised and understood independently of dualistic thought structures. These structures place irrationality in a negative relationship with rationality.

The BFS draws upon qualities that have been defined as 'irrational' within culture and infuses them with a positive spirit. These can be physiological aspects that are or have been considered particular to women's bodies, such as menstruation and creativity, or supernatural, invisible phenomena. She reclaims these positions. She deploys them as a creative force to be harnessed and celebrated.

Rebirth

To be able to die and be reborn is an important tool of the BFS. In later life rebirth becomes the central motif of survival for the BFS. Rebirth first emerges as a concept on the song 'Room for the Life.' In this song rebirth and death are linked to the cultural and biological experience of women to produce life. The possibility of being reborn is fundamentally grounded within the female body and what it is able to *do*.

Historically women have been oppressed by cultural ideologies surrounding motherhood. These have tended to situate women's destinies within their bodies. The BFS's experience of motherhood contradicts this. Like so much of the album, this song provides a portrait of a woman who inhabits an active position of agency and desire. This infuses the female body with autonomy. In the later life of the BFS, extended explorations of the rebirth theme depart from the female body and maternity. However it is really important that this theme is 'born' initially through the womb of womanly experience.

'Room for the Life' is a song about women's resilience. This emerges from the 'room for life' of the womb. The character in the song is reflective of an 'everywoman' that the BFS coaxes into life in the song. She is 'giving birth' to her by providing support through her own 'mothering.' French writer Hélène Cixous writes that, 'There always remains in woman that force which produces/is produced by the other – in particular, the other woman. *In* her, matrix, cradler; herself as giver as mother and child; she is her own sister-daughter.'[37]

This resonates strongly with the behaviour of the BFS in the song. As Cixous says, 'In women there is always more or less of the mother who makes everything all right, who nourishes, and who stands up against separation; a force that will not be cut off but will knock the wind out of the codes.'[38] 'Room for the Life' also celebrates nourishing and life-giving force of the maternal for women. The BFS sings to the woman in the song as sister, daughter and mother. She provides her with support and comfort in all of her melancholy wretchedness.

We first encounter the portrait of the 'everywoman' in 'Room for the Life' when she is isolated, weary and dejected. She sits in her house seemingly waiting for something, or someone, to come and save her. In traditional fairy tales, of course, it is a Prince Charming figure that will come *to* the woman. In 'Room for the Life' it is a fellow woman empowering her to survive and to have the courage to grasp the life, love and desire she may not be aware she can attain for herself. The melody is a gentle piano ballad, comprised predominantly from major chords. These contribute to the soothing atmosphere of the song. Lyrically, the song plays upon particular cultural myths about women's emotional and manipulative nature: 'Hey there you lady in tears/ Do you think that they care if they're real woman?/ They just take it as part of the deal/ Lost in your men and the games you play' (*KI*).

The tearful and emotional state of the 'lady' is suggested to be a norm of female experience, 'They just take it as part of the deal' (*KI*). In the next section the 'woman's' resilience is emphasised: 'Like it or not we were built tough/ Because we're woman' (*KI*). These lines may seem naive. However, the song is about giving 'woman' a power that has traditionally been denied to her in male-defined culture. If there was no mention of such a desire then the song would speedily become a farce of baby rattles, cots and boo-bam drums. These are the toy-like instruments that convey an ambience of the maternal in the chorus. The BFS places woman's maternal capacities next to 'woman' as an actively desiring being. This challenges the stereotypical representations of women when they are mothers. The maternal body is a desexualised body. In the song it is portrayed in a different light.

In the chorus the thematic emergence of rebirth is realised. Importantly it is accessed through the maternal body: 'No, we never die for long/ While we've got that little life to live for' (*KI*). For 'it's hid inside, no, we never die for long/ Oh – woman, two in one/ There's room for a life in your womb, woman/ Inside of you, can be two, woman/ There's room for a life in your womb' (*KI*).

Here 'woman' is equated with life. The life that moves breathes and changes all the time. The womb is the vital organ which makes that life. We are told that '*we never die for long*' (*KI*, italics mine). This 'death' is only ever temporary, with the possibility of being born again inherent in the very idea of 'woman.' It is a critical moment for the song and for the life of the BFS in general. Note the repeated invocation of 'woman.' This is intensified in the chorus but is present in the verses too. It serves to underline the specificity of the address. This is a song that exclusively pertains to women's experiences. It is *for* woman, to enrich her strength and her vision.

The second verse continues the portrait of the everywoman; 'Night after night in the quiet house/ Plaiting her hair by the fire, woman/ With no lover to *free her desire*/ How long do you think she can stick it out' (*KI*). The verse then encourages her to be an active agent of her desire: '*Hey get up on your feet and go get it now*/ Like it or not we keep bouncing back/ Because we're woman' (*KI*, italics mine).

Here the concerns of the woman in the song are far from issues of maternity. What is important is the absent lover who will 'free her desire'. She has to actively go and find it. The woman harbours a desire *independent* of the limited 'options' available to the 70s woman, the options of mother and housewife. Although the song stops short of claiming that *she can free that desire herself*. Other possibilities are intimated beyond those roles and as feminist post-punk band the Au Pairs sang, 'roles give you cramp.'[39] These possibilities move beyond the immediate frame of circumscribed reality for women within male-defined culture. Like so many of the songs of the album, there is no sex-specific address. The absence of indicative pronouns allow for a desire that is largely free from heterosexual expectations.

By the end of the second verse the speaker has returned to the informal address that the song begins with. This time there is a direct call for movement: 'Hey get up on your feet and go get it now!' (*KI*). Although sung in a sweet and gentle tone this statement is a pressing one. It is directed specifically at motivating and mobilising female listeners. The continual stress at the end of the lines on 'woman' further emphasises this. It is meant to trigger in female listeners a recognition and identification with the woman in the song.

Despite 'Room for the Life's aim to liberate the woman in the song, it is easy to understand how it can be interpreted in reactionary ways. Drawing upon maternal imaginaries and power can reinforce the idea that the woman's place is in the home. A number of feminist writers in the 1970s sought to reclaim the maternal as a site of power and resistance. I have already quoted Cixous above, but American poet Adrienne Rich used a similar strategy. These writers sought to revolutionise what they thought of as women's inherently creative powers that could be celebrated through the maternal. They saw this as a way to resist patriarchal ideologies that immobilise women's maternal capacities. There are similar tactics at play on *The Kick Inside*.

To demonstrate some of the 'problems' that this strategy poses, we can return to Reilly's interpretation of the album in his review 'Uncaged Bird.' It seems fair to say that at the time of the record's release male listeners of 'Room for the Life' would not have been 'threatened' by a song that eulogises a role that has kept women in their biologically determined place. As Reilly's review put it: '*Probably the strongest song on the album* is "Room for the Life," which in one way is a call to those still caged tweetie pies and in another is a simple statement of the perils of freedom, liberation and independence in the life of any seventies woman.'[40] Here Reilly's subtle sexism touches upon the tensions and ambiguities of the strategies of the song. It is interesting that he deems it to be the 'strongest on the album.' He interprets it as a warning of the perils of the freedom promised by women's liberation in the 1970s.

In my reading I draw attention to the way the song empowers women to explore and act upon their desire. I want to suggest that the song is more complicated than simply affirming the sanctity of women's maternal role. The ambiguities that the song produces are not surprising given that women writers 'who adopt the mother, or the mother's body, [do so] as an emblem of defiance. They use the maternal to express emblematically the tensions that women experience in their lives.'[41]

The nurturing and supportive role of the BFS in the song is in keeping with Cixous's idea that, as women, 'we are all mothers.' This strategy opens up different possible relational networks. Within male-defined culture women are socialised to direct their desire towards men, rather than at each other. Through the type of 'mothering' dramatised in 'Room for the Life' women's kinship with each other can potentially be reaffirmed. This further creates the possibility for transforming female bonds within culture outside of heterosexual norms.

For the BFS, using the maternal allows her to move between the spaces of death, birth and rebirth. They assure that she will always 'keep bouncing back/ Because we're woman' (*KI*). In 'Room for the Life,' the concept of rebirth is produced through the maternal body of the BFS. It uses the female body as a generative, resilient and creative site. She will depart from this particular aspect of the body later in her life. This will demonstrate how the BFS emerges from the female body but is not reduced to it.

Taboo

The BFS is fascinated by taboos. She tells the stories of bodies, eroticism and desire that would usually remain unspeakable. There are frank expressions of female sexuality and celebrations of women's bodily fluids. They display an urge to release cultural forces that have long been marginalised. These testimonies to deviance are figured in intensely erotic ways.

The title track to the album, 'The Kick Inside,' demonstrates this. Clearly an important and symbolic track, it was chosen to provide the name for the whole collection of songs. In many ways it invokes the maternal metaphor described in the rebirth section. It fuses birth, femaleness and creativity. However, when listening to the song 'The Kick Inside' it could be easy to miss what the song is in fact about. The song does celebrate pregnancy, like the previous song 'Room for the Life.' This pregnancy is the result of an incestuous relationship between a brother and a sister. 'The kick inside' is the consequence of their intercourse.

Incest has been a mainstay of Western myth from Sophocles to Freud. It has remained a taboo subject evoking horror and dread. Nevertheless, Kate Bush thought it was a ripe subject for a pop song. She explained:

> The song 'The Kick Inside,' the title track, was inspired by

> a traditional folk song and it was an area that I wanted to explore because it's one that is really untouched and that is one of incest. There are so many songs about love, but they are always on such an obvious level. This song is about a brother and a sister who are in love and the sister becomes pregnant by her brother. And because it is so taboo and unheard of, she kills herself in order to preserve her brother's name in the family. The actual song is in fact the suicide note. The sister is saying 'I'm doing it for you' and 'don't worry, I'll come back to you someday.'[42]

The incestuous relationship on 'The Kick Inside' is portrayed in an erotic and poetic manner. The romance of the brother and sister is taken seriously. The lines suggest a familiar family intimacy: 'This kicking here inside makes me leave you behind/ No more under the quilt to keep you warm' (*KI*). This intimacy is something that brother and sister share: 'You and me on the bobbing knee/ Didn't we cry at that old mythology he'd read' (*KI*).

The song highlights the romanticism of their encounter: 'I pull down my lace and the chintz/ Oh, do you know you have the face of a genius/ I'll send your love to Zeus/ Oh, by the time you read this, I'll be well in touch' (*KI*). This is coupled with an intense celebration of sexuality: 'I'm giving it all in a moment or two/ I'm giving it all in a moment for you/ I'm giving it all, giving it, giving it - giving it' (*KI*).

'The Kick Inside' departs from the tale of 'Lucy Wan,' the Child Ballad from England and Scotland which the song is based on, in significant ways. Usually the story of 'Lucy Wan' is told in the brother's voice.[43] However, the BFS tells the tale from the sister's perspective. This gives the Lucy character a voice that is marginalised within 'Lucy Wan.' Usually, it is the tragedy and pathos of the brother's situation that generates the dramatic energy of the song. In 'The Kick Inside' it is the romance and love between the brother and the sister which is told from Lucy's perspective.

In 'Lucy Wan,' Lucy is granted a mere four lines in which to voice her perception and feelings about the situation. When she does, her brother cuts her head off, and her body, into three bits: 'Oh I ail and I ail dear brother, she said,/ I'll tell you the reason why, /There is a child between my two sides,/ Between you, dear Billy, and I.'[44]

There is not a glimmer of the lace, chintz and romance of 'The Kick Inside' and likewise, in the later version we do not know that Lucy is brutally murdered. Instead the song is placed in the context of her desire and childlike memories. In 'Lucy Wan' it is the misery of the brother whose 'good broad sword/ That hung down by his knees'[45] is prioritised. There is a lack of grief expressed by the mother when she hears that it is not the greyhound's blood that covers her son's sword, but her daughter's. 'The Kick Inside' does re-use the brother's parting phrase 'When the sun and the moon rise over hill.'[46] This line sums up the impossibility of a peaceful resolution without a gruesome death: 'I will come home again, but not until/ The sun and the moon meet on yon hill' (*KI*).

On 'The Kick Inside' the drama, pathos and perspective of the story is altered to reflect the sister's experience. Highlighting the active female voice is consistent with the strategies of other songs on the album. These create similar active spaces for female protagonists. From these spaces, the woman can express her desire on her own terms. This enables women to leave a more substantial mark within the structures of storytelling that would normally exclude her.

On a surface level, 'The Kick Inside' appears to be destructive of this active female power. However, understanding the story's roots within folk tradition provides an alternative perspective. In 'The Kick Inside' the sister is making the *choice* to kill herself. She 'steals' the active voice and phrase from her brother and reverses their positions. It is she who is leaving never to return. She is not reduced to an object as in the earlier version of the tale with her 'fair body in three'[47] parts. Death is not forced upon her. There is still, of course, an element of complicity with male cultural power. Her brother's 'good name' will be preserved as a result of her suicide. Nevertheless, the aspect of choice is always highlighted in Lucy's actions. They also emphasise the protagonist's strong desire for her brother. As problematic as this is, it offers a justification for her choice. This was nowhere to be found in the earlier version.

The BFS is fascinated by taboos and refuses to remain silent about them. 'The Kick Inside' is evidence of this. By engaging with taboo subjects such as incest, she moves the boundaries of what is permissive. She leaves listeners feeling implicated in difficult situations. She does not re-instate taboo but revels in it. No area is too sacred or profane for the BFS. She will continue to break taboos during the course of her life.

The next stage of the journey

We have now reached an important point in the life of the BFS: she has been born. From *The Kick Inside* the BFS takes with her an armoury of weapons. These will allow her to move through the world of her own creation. They emerge from the female body with its generative power but do not have to stay there. They carry the power to be multiple, irrational, fluid; the power to have a voice and desire and to be reborn. The only certain thing that the BFS takes with her on the journey is that she will change.

In next stage of the BFS's journey, we embark upon a different arena, the follow up to *The Kick Inside*, *Lionheart*. This will see the BFS take on further different forms. She will experiment with gender and sexuality. She will re-negotiate her own whiteness, Englishness and the histories of colonialism. She will be camp and nostalgic. She will not stay the same.

Lionheart and the Queer Life of the BFS

I know I'm artificial
But don't put the blame on me
I was reared with appliances
In a consumer society

X – Ray Spex 'Art – I – ficial'[1]

Lionheart is a queer affair. Gone are the obsessions with the female body that preoccupy the BFS on *The Kick Inside*. The change was quick too. *Lionheart* was released a mere 11 months after the appearance of the BFS on the world's stage. Many saw the album as rushed and the result of music industry pressure.

Nevertheless, the BFS more than holds her own ground on it. She revels in the pleasure of performance. She explores themes through role play, acting, scripts and stories. She draws upon the theatricality of entertainment and show business. The musical arrangements are quasi-orchestral, grand and hyperbolic. They communicate an atmosphere of melodrama and parody. Through a combination of these things, the queer life of the BFS is released. She takes on new forms.

Many of the songs on *Lionheart* are based around the idea of acting and performance. Bush biographer Rob Jovanovich suggests that the album was to form the theatrical inspiration for the 'Tour of Life,' the only tour that Bush would perform in her life in 1979 (a tour that would stage the BFS in live action). He states that 'she had wanted the new material to fit in with her advanced vision of what that tour should be: a totally theatrical experience unlike the usual rock and pop shows of her contemporaries.'[2]

Lionheart, more than any other album where the BFS lives and breathes, was music made with performance in mind. This lends the BFS a particular license to explore different identities other than just being herself. Within the freedom of performance it is easier to inhabit and explore new characters. Theatre has always offered a culturally acceptable space where transgression can be explored, particularly in relation to gender. Think of all the men who played women on the stage in Shakespeare's time.[3] Theatre gives you space to be what you are not. Performance allows you to be what you could be - if only you had the chance: What you may become.

Challenging Gender Through Performance

The *Lionheart* era saw the BFS challenge many boundaries of gendered 'correctness.' The most dramatic example of this comes from a Christmas Special TV programme in 1979.[4] Here she performed what would later become the B-side to the single 'Babooshka,' 'Ran-Tan Waltz.' This extraordinary footage depicts the BFS in full male drag (including an impressive beard) dancing with two other men, one of whom, is dressed in a baby costume. The dance performance typically interprets the song, which is a first-person narrative by a man who has been deserted by 'his' woman and is left 'holding the baby.'[5]

The routine shows the BFS shift and jolt as she manoeuvres between and over her dance partners. 'She' presents an exaggerated yet fragile masculinity. In the middle of the routine she is turned upside down. Her trademark flowing long brown hair falls out from under her cap. It stays there throughout the rest of the song. This dance move sabotages the performance of gender she is presenting. It foregrounds the constructed and performed nature of masculinity.

This moment of gender parody corresponds to American philosopher Judith Butler's ideas about drag. Butler draws attention to how drag performances imitate gender. In doing so, they reveal how the binary gender system of male and female is made up of a series of imitations. Drag *visibly* questions the idea that there is an original or essential gender that belongs to 'men' and 'women.' It 'reveals that the original identity after which gender fashions itself is an imitation without an origin.'[6]

Gender roles, Butler argues, only become a normal part of day-to-day life through the 'stylized repetition of acts.'[7] That is, as subjects we take on styles of gender by repeating them. As there is no original gender and gender is always an imitation, these repetitions tend to miss the mark. In day-to-day life, most people perform their gender badly. We fail to be that 'perfect woman' or 'perfect man.' By taking this idea to excess, drag performances reveal the imitated quality of gender more visibly to people. When we see a drag performance, it creates an opportunity for us to see that gender is constructed and able to change.

This is what the BFS does in the performance for 'Ran-Tan Waltz.' 'Her' over the top beard makes absolutely no attempt to appear natural. As the hair falls out of the cap we know that she is pretending to be a man, and is radically failing at that! None of it, in the strictest sense, is believable. We know we are watching an imitation and we gain enjoyment from this. This is part of the 'pleasure [and] giddiness of the performance,' as it presents the conditions where the 'recognition of a radical contingency in the relation between sex and gender'[8] can emerge. That is, we gain a sense from watching drag that masculinity 'belongs' no more to a male body than it does to a female, and vice versa. It makes gender unstable. Boys can be girls and girls can be boys. The BFS uses these queer strategies in *Lionheart*.

The BFS's androgyny

The gendered flavour of *Lionheart* is androgynous. This propels the BFS's performances. On the front cover she appears dressed in a lion's costume that conceals the contours of her body. This is suggestive of gender ambiguity. She masquerades as a pretty young man. Her use of make-up and exaggerated hair crimping makes it look like a wig.

The whole look serves to recall the heyday of the 'glam' era of the early to mid-70s, in which many male performers 'feminised' themselves through their use of costume. The BFS stares aggressively and seductively at the camera in a predatory, but ultimately camp, fashion.

In *Lionheart* the crossing of gender boundaries and the communication of camp is found in a number of places. These include the BFS's voice itself as well as the narratives presented in the songs. We should remember that the BFS's voice is 'Sapphonic.' That is, it can slide through a large number of vocal registers:

> The extreme range in one female voice from richly dark deep chest tones to piercingly clear high falsetto, and its defective break at crossing register borders, produces an effect I call sonic cross dressing – a merging rather than splitting of 'butch' authority and 'femme' ambiguity, an acceptance and integration of male and female.[9]

The BFS is famous for her piercingly high vocals. On *Lionheart* her vocals seem at times uncomfortably high pitched. What is often overlooked is how deep her voice can also become. Its aggressive and macho qualities and how she can often slide between these two extreme pitches within a song.

Wood describes the 'Sapphonic voice' as one that is 'a transvestic enigma, belonging to neither male nor female as constructed.'[10] In the BFS's voice alone, a case of 'sonic cross-dressing' is found. This integrates both male and female positions – a vocal space that enables the subject to occupy a number of positions along a gendered vocal spectrum. The very nature of the BFS's singing voice is the power to intrude upon supposedly stable gendered positions. These would normatively serve to demarcate and reinstate the fixed boundaries of gender roles (i.e. men have low voices and women have high voices).

The BFS's 'transvestic' voice destabilises cultural norms because of the range it can encompass. It is a vital tool of negotiation and creation for her. In a very functional way the BFS's primary instrument enabled her to depart from gentle, stereotypically feminine music. Her vocal flexibility enabled her to move into a 'masculine' space - even if only to use it as a parodic device.

'In Search of Peter Pan' and the transgender astronaut

It seems no coincidence that a figure such as Peter Pan should feature prominently on *Lionheart*. The album celebrates sliding between genders and bodies in performance. It does so in order to stall the inevitability of stereotypical gendered fates. The figure of Peter Pan represents resistance to the norms of adulthood with its conventions and rules. These can oppress individuals by imposing narrow and segregated gender roles.

Peter Pan escapes the adult world precisely because he can (despite the use of the 'he' pronoun) escape gender. Due to his androgyny he has the advantage of experiencing both genders. The BFS privileges this version of Peter Pan that has come to suggest the possibility of indeterminate gender within the Western cultural imaginary. In traditional and contemporary versions of the play Peter Pan, the Pan figure is often played by a woman. It is worth remembering that the Pan of J.M. Barrie's novel assumes a traditionally masculine and authoritarian leadership role.[11]

Peter Pan is an appropriate figure through which to express the gendered anxiety of the BFS. 'In Search of Peter Pan' is told from the perspective of a speaker who is on the cusp of growing up. Their gender is not stated and shifts in a fluid manner in the song. Like Peter Pan they remain in an indeterminate gendered state: 'It's been such a long week,/ So much crying./ I no longer see a future/ *I've been told, when I get older/ That I'll understand it all/ But I'm not sure if I want to*' (*LH*, italics mine).

The last three lines of the opening verse speak in the voice of the child. They have been told by authority figures that they will have to accept the rules of society when they grow up. In doing so they may lose large parts of themselves. They are not sure if they want to. These lines articulate a resistance to growing up as defined by the straight world.

Queer writer Judith Halberstam suggests that this is a form of queer resistance. By refusing to grow up, this demonstrates a 'politics of refusal – the refusal to grow up and enter the hetero-normative adulthoods implied by these concepts of progress and maturity.'[12] The refusal to grow up is a refusal to have kids and get a mortgage. To be normal, just like everyone else. It is the freedom to have a fluid age, to be both child and adult and shift between these states. A similar resistance is articulated by the BFS in this song.

In the second verse the speaker is consoled by their grandmother. She chides them for being 'too sensitive' (*LH*) which is typically feminine behaviour. The speaker says this 'makes me sad./ She makes me feel like an old man' (*LH*), a line that also conjures up interesting gendered confusions. The chorus is equally destabilising: 'When, when I am a man/ I will be an astronaut/ And find Peter Pan' (*LH*). This yearning is exclusive to men. Only when the speaker is a *man* can they grow up to be astronaut. This yearning is emphasised by a repeated and insistent 'when,' accentuated by how this statement is delivered - rising up then trailing off into a cosmic imaginary space.

The song also creates space for transgendered subjectivities can emerge, if the meaning of the 'trans' prefix is taken to mean movement across multiple sites of gender. These transform gender identity as she is a little girl wishing, wanting, waiting until she can become a man. This will enable her to realise her dreams. The figure of the astronaut here becomes a crucial metaphor on which to pin the dream of action, movement, flight, daring and imagination.

'In Search of Peter Pan' also contains male narcissism: 'Dennis loves to look in the mirror/ He tells me that he is beautiful' (*LH*). This later becomes a larger allusion to homoeroticism, 'He's got a photo/ Of his hero/ He keeps it under his pillow' (*LH*). The speaker, on the other hand, has a pin-up of Peter Pan. They 'found...in a locket, I hide it in my pocket' (*LH*) which is a piece of jewellery traditionally worn by women. This further confuses the boundaries of gender in the song. In both cases there is an element of secrecy and shame about coveting these pictures.

One is hidden under a pillow. The other is hidden in a pocket. This may simply be part of the 'game' of being a child. It could also indicate an awareness of the gendered and sexual transgressions that the song dramatises, and the desires that these statements make publicly known.

'In Search of Peter Pan' offers a subtle yet convincing argument for the right of all people to be free from the gendered expectations that society places upon them. The use of 'When you wish upon a star' (*LH*) from the Disney film *Pinocchio* at the end of the song stresses the plaintive innocence of this statement. It is connected to the 'Pan' mantra quoted in the chorus: 'Second Star on the right/ Straight on 'til morning' (*LH*). The closing message of the song affirms that it 'Makes no difference who you are' (*LH*). This makes the wish that all people, regardless of class, gender and race should have the freedom to realise their wildest of dreams.

In 'In Search of Peter Pan' the BFS uses fluid and shifting gender techniques. She does this in order to critique restrictive hetero-normative and patriarchal gender roles and conceptions of time. The song is saturated with the pain of binary gender's limitations and yearns to escape them. It privileges the imagination as the arena where this flight can be achieved.

The campy theatrical artifice of the BFS

The BFS often expresses female masculinity. She does this using camp performance. This is the next stage of the BFS's journey. She parades her (ef)feminacy throughout *Lionheart*. This effeminised masculinity is important. It 'affords us a glimpse of how masculinity is constructed as masculinity.'[13] Like drag, when masculinity is embodied by women or femininity by men, it allows us to see the ways in which it is constructed. This is either through cultural codes and the adoption of styles that are repeated. The BFS's use of camp involves an interesting twist of vocal and subjective transvestism. She can be a woman performing as a man who in turn is adopting, parodying and inhabiting female characteristics. The way the BFS turns gender over on Lionheart is *multiple*.

The performance on the album resonates with a certain type of male homosexual culture. The BFS is still heralded as a higher class of camp gay (male) icon for the twentieth and twenty-first centuries. Nathan Evans wrote in gay newspaper *The Pink Paper*: 'mainstream gay culture has Kylie or Madonna. But Kate's fantastically camp. She's a one-off eccentric. I really don't think her image was constructed in an ironic way. She was just being herself.'[14] The *genuinely* eccentric aspect of the BFS places her apart from the plasticity of mainstream and commodified gay culture. The BFS is just being herself. She is authentically camp.

There has been much contention over the definition and meaning of 'camp.' Most consistently, camp has been associated with 'a mode of performance that exposes as artifice what passes as natural.'[15] The BFS's camp can't really be 'authentic' (unless she is authentically artificial). As a political tool, camp has been put to use to query compulsory heterosexuality within culture. To question the idea that heterosexuality is 'natural.' Richard Dyer defines camp in the following way:

> Camp can make us see that what art and the media give us are not the Truth or Reality but fabrications, particular ways of talking about the world, particular understandings and feelings of the way that life is. Art and the media don't give us life as it really is – how could they ever? – but only life as artists and producers think it is. Camp, by drawing attention to the artifices employed by artists, can constantly remind us that what we are seeing is only *a view of life*. This doesn't stop us enjoying it, but it does stop us believing what we are shown too readily.[16]

Dyer defines camp as a strategy. It is a critical perception that enables people to challenge singular ways of seeing the world. Importantly, Dyer stresses that this does not curtail the enjoyment of what is being experienced. Nevertheless it offers a space for the reader of a cultural text to resist its messages. Camp remains sceptical of accepted norms and what is seen as 'authentic' or 'natural.' It engages with artifice as a device, in order to reveal the artificiality of reality. It is a 'style that favours "exaggeration," artifice and extremity... [it] exists in tension with popular culture, commercial culture or consumerist culture.'[17]

Christopher Isherwood's definition of 'high camp' is appropriate to describe the camp of the BFS. He writes of the decadence and seriousness of high camp. 'You camp about something you take seriously. You're not making fun *of* it, you're making fun *out* of it. You're expressing what's basically serious to you in terms of fun and artifice and elegance.'[18] Isherwood might just as well have been listening to *Lionheart* when he wrote this. There is often a gravity to the songs that co-exists with the more humorous aspects. These revel in artificiality – the storytelling of the BFS – and elegance; the music and vocal performance are well constructed and executed. The BFS uses camp to challenge many of the things within culture that posture as natural. Embracing artifice through the BFS is a key to changing perceptions of the cultural world.

These strategies can be found on the single released from the album, 'Wow.' Based in the ruthless world of show-business, the song contains a teasing critique of the entertainment industry. It makes fun of its routines and the roles people have to play in order to get anywhere within it. Equally, the song might be referring to the roles played in everyday life. These are also scripts that when learnt and repeated can fall into predictable patterns. 'We know all our lines so well, ah-ha,/ We've said them so many times,/ Time and time again,/ Line and line again' (*LH*).

The song gently plays upon the hypocrisy of the industry and glamorises failure in the face of flattery. It tells the story of the young gay man who'll never 'Be that movie queen/ He's too busy hitting the Vaseline' (*LH*). In the video the BFS pouts at the camera knowingly and spanks her bottom when singing this line. This cheekily suggests she knows the pleasure of anal intercourse.

Perverse! The BFS is perverse (of course anal sex is not perverse!) Even more so as the conceptual world of *Lionheart* is characterised by a childish, dreamlike wonder. This co-exists with the 'adult' fascination with desire and sexuality expressed on *The Kick Inside*. This perverse tendency on *Lionheart* is, at times, hilariously perverted. 'The more I think about sex the better it gets' (*LH*) the BFS sings on 'Symphony in Blue' in high-femme tones, cooing in a voice that is part girl-child, drag queen and temptress. While the deep hushed tones of 'In the Warm Room' should only be described as a school boy's absurd fantasy: 'In the warm room/ You'll fall into her like a pillow./ Her thighs are soft as marshmallows./ Say hello/ To the soft musk of her hollows' (*LH*). The BFS is a seductress. She leads people astray with her delectably dirty ways. She is ridiculous and sexy in the same turn. She is unmistakably camp.

The chorus of 'Wow,' with the repeated 'Wow,' communicates the wonder and magic of showbiz. The ambivalent 'unbelievable' at the end points to the tension between fantasy and reality that theatre and performance embody. The chorus also demonstrates the vocal cross dressing of the BFS that Wood describes in 'Sapphonics.' 'Wow' oscillates across a scale in its repetitions. It begins in the middle register, soaring impossibly high, then low, before finishing astoundingly with the high release of the final 'unbelievable.' The song comments on the artifice of acting. It means to assure those credulous viewers and listeners that what they see before them is not real. It points to a will that hovers between wanting and not wanting the spell to be broken: 'When the actor reaches his death/ You know it's not for real, he just holds his breath' (*LH*).

The enduring tone and feeling of *Lionheart* is of outrageous, histrionic male camp and theatricality. As Bush commented, referring to the inspiration for 'Wow,' 'there are an awful lot of homosexuals in the business. But that is just an observation, not a criticism.'[19] Camp is found best on the two songs that close the album, 'Coffee Homeground' and 'Hammer Horror.' These songs both display all the fun that can be gained from engaging with elegance and artifice. 'Coffee Homeground' opens with swaggering and swooping tones that envelop the listener like overbearing plumes. The music evokes entering a cellar or a boardroom. The atmosphere sets the mood of the song which tells the story of a man who poisons his guests by putting belladonna in their food and drink.

At the time it was described as 'a humorous aspect of paranoia really and we sort of done it [sic] in a Brechtian style, the old sort of German Vibe to try and bring across the humour side of it.'[20] The song certainly conjures the decadent aspects of 1920s Berlin. It has lurching polka rhythms, and an isolated cymbal clash that delivers the punch line between the stop/start of the music.

Despite giving the appearance of being created by a large orchestra, the sound of the horns and ethereal flutes are in fact made by a synthesizer. Developed in the late 1970s, it is the ultimate artificial instrument. This is another way that artifice creeps into the album's body. This makes it appear more elaborate than it actually is. Synthesizers feature on the campest songs on the album – 'Wow,' 'Coffee' and 'Hammer' – while the other songs use more traditional instruments. This is no easy coincidence when considering how the atmosphere is created. What we think of as 'natural' instruments are in fact programmed and simulated sounds.

'Coffee Homeground' could also be read aloud as a script, written and performed with a carry on-esque spanking and flick of the wrist: 'Offer me a chocolate,/ No thank you, spoil my diet, *know your game!*' (*LH*, italics mine). Importantly, the song is humorous. This is all the more surprising given that it is about murder. It is in keeping with Isherwood's definition of high camp that makes fun *out* of something as opposed to *of* something. There is a full sense of theatricality and entertainment. The song itself becomes a kind of play. Instruments and extra voices function as characters. The BFS is often embroiled in complex little stories. As she tells them they construct their own dramatic world.

The final song on the album, 'Hammer Horror,' is another example of this. The song opens with an extended hold on one note. A wall of noise builds anticipation and intrigue before a cymbal crashes. A piano is then struck up and down the scale. A synthesizer flourishes in the background before the singing begins and the focus is placed on the voice, bass guitar and piano. It is appropriate to talk of this song and

'Coffee Homeground' as elaborate and orchestral. Tremendous care has gone into perfecting each particular part of the song. 'Hammer Horror,' despite its elegance and beautiful melodrama, is an odd pop song. There are a number of structural changes and mutations it undergoes along its journey. Ron Moy makes a similar point: 'it is much too fragmented in structure to be a successful commercial single.'[21] But released it was, like so many of the BFS's appearances in public, she refused to fit in and forced people to acknowledge her.

Like 'Coffee,' 'Hammer Horror' is theatrical. It is akin to a mini-play or musical. The use of the BFS's voice and instruments contribute to this. The BFS sings in a low voice to deliver the main story. Her high pitched voice is used to echo, emphasise and build the melodrama of the song. Her voices impress upon listeners from a number of different places and positions simultaneously. It sings the multiplicity of the BFS. This is communicated through the use of voices and sounds.

Like much of *Lionheart*, 'Hammer Horror' is based in the world of theatre. 'The song is not about, as many think, Hammer Horror films. It is about an actor and his friend.'[22] The friend dies just as he is about to take the main part in the play, *The Hunchback of Notre Dame*. The speaker of the song has to take his place. He is haunted by the ghost, 'all I want to do is forget you, friend' (*LH*). Like 'Kashka from Baghdad' which we will look at later, a connection between male homosexual love and death is strongly alluded to: 'Who calls me from the other side,/ Of the street?/ And who taps me on the shoulder?/ I turn around, but you're gone' (*LH*). 'Hammer Horror' ends with the sound of large gong cymbal. This signifies the closing of the curtains on the play - and indeed the whole album.

The presence of 'high camp' can be detected everywhere within *Lionheart*. Through the use of voices, themes, instruments, humour and parody, it is used as a strategy to explore, and ultimately to expose, the artifice of fantasy, reality and all that postures as 'natural' within culture. This use of camp is more than just frivolous fun. It is a tactic to negotiate the narrow position that the BFS, with her female body, was confined to. It becomes an important part of the conceptual armoury of the BFS.

The next part of the journey of the BFS shows yet another side to her. Remember she is a shape-shifter and has many different sides. The BFS has already proved herself to be a bit of a vanguard in relation to gender and sexuality. However she is also prone to perpetuating stereotypical ideas about Nationalism and race. The next part of the journey will show her involved in mythologizing ideas about Englishness and Nationalism. This is an important twist in the tale of the BFS and will affect her future movements.

The BFS as England's good daughter

'Everything I do is very English and I think that's one reason why I've broken through to a lot of countries.'[23] In her early life the BFS strongly connects herself to an English identity. It is part of everything she does. It is her unique selling point in the global market. *Lionheart* invokes Richard the Lionheart and Britain's long and continuing history of colonialism. In doing so she aligns herself, with a certain amount of naiveté, to this history. This has implications for the future life of the BFS.

There is a significant difference between the BFS of *The Kick Inside* and the BFS of *Lionheart*. This difference can be found in her claiming of an English identity. The BFS of *The Kick Inside* is unmarked by such essentialist characteristics that tie her down to a particular place or history. She draws upon the female body but crucially she is not reduced to it. She uses that body to generate difference. She is universal, an 'everywoman.' Of course she is not perfect. However, she is definitely more interested in taking down borders rather than reaffirming them. The BFS of *Lionheart* on the other hand, articulates a specific allegiance to England. She defines herself as English; she resides within a territory. It is part of everything she does.

This is a crucial shift in the life of the BFS. It sets up a boundary that had previously not been relevant in her life. It will affect the way she relates to others. By imagining herself as English, the BFS inherits histories of nationalism, colonialism and racism. She appropriates 'othered' cultures through Orientalist devices. The BFS cannot remove herself from these histories. She is implicated within them. They stick to her. This will affect how she speaks about what is different from 'the English,' what is different from her. Instead of embodying difference, the BFS comes to objectify it. She distances herself from difference and exoticises it. She creates an inside and an outside where she holds privilege. She no longer is the other.

The BFS always has a cultural context

The BFS does not exist in a vacuum. She always exists at particular moments in history. These moments shapes what she can say, do and how she says it. When she first made her appearance in the late 1970s, race relations in Britain were a contentious issue. Roger Sabin argues that it was a 'period more tense in this regard than at any point since the Second World War.'[24] The late 1970s saw the growing popularity of the National Front, the biggest of Britain's fascist parties. By 1976 it had become the fourth largest political party in Britain. In the more mainstream political parties too, the race 'question' became the key to winning political power. Sabin asserts that:

> The Conservative Party, then in opposition, proved anxious to steal the NF's fire by making race a key issue. The Labour government itself was far from non-racist, and made little effort to tackle racism in other organs of the state, (especially in the police and the courts) or indeed in the employment market or in schools.[25]

1976 saw many Asian immigrants who held British passports come to live in the UK. They had been expelled from Uganda, Kenya and Malawi. Political agendas at the time defined these people as a threat to the 'British' way of life. This was seen to be under attack. Right-wing political discourses about immigration often talk about purity of white British identity being 'swamped' and 'contaminated' by the arrival of new immigrant communities. Such discourses are motivated by the white supremacist idea that Britain is a white country and that this whiteness should be protected. Whiteness is seen as something pure that can be kept separate. Border laws are the legal expression of this racist ideology.

Lionheart's pastoral idealisation of English identity would have appealed to the people who felt that the traditional ways of English life were under threat. The BFS's presentation as a 'good English girl' or 'England's favourite daughter' played right into the hands of popular consciousness. Terry Slater from EMI commented that the BFS 'is a real English girl, she's from the roots of Great Britain. It's not a gimmick or produced. She's the first really *English* girl singer for a long time.'[26] A large part of the BFS's appeal is the 'purity' of her Englishness. Emerging from the roots of the land, she is authentic, natural, pure and uncontaminated.

This is not all just presentation. The BFS's Englishness emerges from her musical inspirations, which colour the songs. Moy's book-length study of Bush outlines what he sees as the 'fundamentally English world that the artist inhabits.'[27] He connects her musical influences with the classical English pastoral tradition of artists such as Elgar, Delius (who has a song named after him on *Never for Ever*), Butterworth, Grainger and Vaughan Williams. Fred Vermorel's book, *Kate Bush: And The Strange Art of Pop*, published in 1983 takes the ideas of roots pretty seriously. The book is a genealogical account of Bush's family tree. It stretches as far back as her 'pagan and savage Saxon roots through 1,400 years in the "witch country" Essex,'[28] up to her immediate family history.

Within the BFS's life she evokes 'a range of white ethnicities, including (olde) English, British and Celtic... [which] invite slippage between, for instance, English and British, or Irish and Celtic.'[29] In the first three albums these white ethnicities remain grounded in English (read British) national, ethnic and racial identity. It was not until 1982's

The Dreaming that Irish instruments and sounds came to feature prominently in her life. It is plausible to suggest that at the time *Lionheart* was released in 1978, the audience would have not considered the BFS to be anything other than representing, and speaking about, an English tradition and cultural heritage: 'I think she's very English, as in Anglo-Saxon with all the olde world and fairie connotations. Knights of the Round Table. Stonehenge. Burning Witches. That sort of thing. I don't see her as being modern at all.'[30]

The BFS 'can be seen to present a nostalgic kind of nationality/ ethnicity that draws on essentialist notions.'[31] This type of nostalgia can be found on the song 'Oh England My Lionheart.' The inspiration for the song emerges from the 'very heavy emphasis on nostalgia that is very strong in England. People really do it a lot, you know, like "I remember the war and..." You know it's very much a part of our attitudes to life that *we live in the past*.'[32] This nostalgia creates an idealised sense of home. It eulogises wholeness and security. The handwritten lyrics on the sleeve notes (all the other lyrics are typed) create an effect of uniqueness and honesty. It is seen to 'endorse the spontaneous sincerity of the song.'[33] They can also be seen to fit in with the childlike innocence of the album. The song is meant to encourage an intimate reaction. Above all it is about love that comes from a heart faithful to the roots and monuments of the land.

'Oh England My Lionheart' begins with a portrait of an England that has been restored to peace after the Second World War. England is the mother country to whose 'garden' 'we' can return to be comforted and healed. The militarism and violence of the war departs. 'The soldiers soften' (*LH*), the BFS is 'in your garden fading fast in your arms' (*LH*). The air raid shelters are now benignly covered with 'blooming clover.' 'Flapping umbrellas fill the lanes' (*LH*) as the rain pours down.

As is common with the BFS, in a song she inhabits a character and tells the story from their perspective. She uses a situation as a vehicle to explore different ideas and viewpoints. This song is told 'from the perspective of a dying pilot shortly after the end of World War II.'[34] When she performed the song as part of 'The Tour of Life', the BFS wore a pilot's costume as she sat on a swing, cooing into the microphone. On the tour it was part of the show's finale, being the penultimate song (she closed with 'Wuthering Heights').

As well as embodying nostalgia towards English culture, 'Oh England my Lionheart' displays a fascination with loss, death and departure. This further underlines the mourning of a generation that is passing. The pilot's last observations become the conduit of this message. This adds a tone of desperation to the chorus of 'Oh England my Lionheart/ I don't want to go' (*LH*).

The BFS will go on in the song 'Army Dreamers' to comment on the limited roles available for men to play within patriarchal culture. There she presents a more rigid critique of the wasteful role of 'soldier' within a more contemporary context. 'Army Dreamers' also displays a sympathetic attitude towards masculinity. It encourages men to be more emotional. The song suggests this will enable men to reject the prescribed roles that are presented as 'natural' within patriarchal culture.

'Oh England My Lionheart,' on the other hand, is still infatuated with the heroism of soldiers. The soldier in the Second World War was one who protected their homeland from invasion. In British culture this celebration of the Second World War is far enough in the past to have been mythologized by countless war films and books. There is a widespread acceptance of the gentlemanly heroism that soldiers were supposed to embody.

The futility of the pilot's death does still creep though in the song. Final memories of his experiences pass before his eyes. Last kisses pass his lips. He meets his final communion with his homeland, symbolised by the English garden: 'Give me one kiss in appleblossom,/ Give me one wish and I'd be wassailing/ In the orchard my English Rose/ Or with my Shepherd who'll bring me home' (*LH*).

The lyrics are a dying person's final wishes. It is a person religiously in love with the characteristics of his homeland. There is not the sense that this *personal* death is unnecessary (a message which firmly comes across in a song like 'Army Dreamers'). Rather the death is firmly romanticised in a way that celebrates its peaceful end. The individual tragedy of the pilot's death is not the overwhelming message of the song. He comes to embody the death of a pure, genteel, chivalrous and heroic England. It is through his body and words that the crisis of memory, nostalgia and yearning is dramatised. Through his eyes there is one last chance to see the old England before it disappears.

The BFS positions herself as a male character in order to tell the story of 'Oh England My Lionheart.' However her sympathy with the character arises less from his stunning virility – his ability to colonise, control and conquer - than from his gentlemanly heroism. Not only is there a sense of nostalgia communicated in the song for the loss of stable and coherent cultural values, but also for such 'gentlemanly' values as honesty, valour and self-sacrifice. The song aims to celebrate heroism. 'Lionheart' 'sorta means hero, and I think hero is a very cliched [sic] word, so I thought *Lionheart* would be a bit different.'[35]

'Oh England My Lionheart' is an intimate communion with a dying hero. His thoughts and feelings are attached to the buildings and gardens of England. The song is punctuated with references to cultural heritage and stories that have emerged from the English landscape. There is an enduring aspect to this culture: 'You read me Shakespeare on the Rolling Thames,/ That old River Poet that never, ever ends,/ Our thumping hearts hold the Ravens in,/ And keep the tower from tumbling' (*LH*).

The figure of Shakespeare represents the heritage of English cultural achievements. His work is the embodiment of a legacy that will not, and cannot, be erased. The words he wrote are a fixture in the English language. They are emblematic of cultural survival: 'That old River Poet that never, ever ends' (*LH*). The architecture of England is also portrayed as being kept alive through the impassioned 'thumping hearts' of the people. What is missing from the song is how the sovereignty of English culture is maintained by subjugating others. Not least the countries that immediately surround it. The continual slippage between

'British' and 'English' underlines the dominance of 'England' over other parts of the 'United Kingdom.' The UK is an island which has colonised difference into itself.

As the BFS sings 'Oh England My Lionheart/ I don't want to go' (*LH*) she cannot let go of this idealised, pure, and culturally perfect England. Like any kind of faith – imagined as they always are, no matter how real it may seem – love and belief are central components of its ability to survive. And what is more real than writing, buildings and the land itself, particularly if we know that these things always outlive people?

These ideas in themselves are not, perhaps, damaging. Nationalism becomes damaging when it is used to assert racial and cultural superiority. When it is exclusive and demarcates boundaries. It can be damaging when this identity is used to unite people essentially through nationalistic characteristics and is underpinned by racist ideologies. The BFS is plaintively naïve and honest in expressing her love and loyalty. Nevertheless she is still implicated in propagating a precious, but damaging, myth. 'Oh England, My Lionheart' is still evocative of such songs like 'There'll always be an England,' described as 'a great song; now very hated by the British Left.'[36] 'There'll always be an England/ While there's a country lane/ Wherever there's a cottage small/ Beside a field of grain.'[37]

'Oh England My Lionheart' does undermine the more aggressive aspects of English nationalism that were dominant in political subcultures (the National Front) and music subcultures (fascist punk) of the late 1970s. This can be found in the music to the song. In contrast to the majority of the songs on the album, the musical accompaniment is minimally orchestrated. It floats reflectively with a gentle and lilting tone. The layers of voices used in the chorus do not conflict with each other in motion, direction or tone. They lightly affirm the song's message. The song is a madrigal and is part of an amatory and pastoral tradition. The inclusion of 'the shepherd who'll bring me home' (*LH*) situates it within this context.

The instruments used on the record are piano, recorder and harpsichord. The piano is a domestic instrument (albeit a middle-class one) and the recorder is an instrument that children learn to play in school. This again underlines the ingenuous impulse of the song. In addition, harpsichord can be seen to invoke the musical heritage of England as it was an instrument popular in Renaissance Britain. The gentleness and simplicity of the song can thus be seen as a challenge to the macho, patriarchal nationalism prevalent in the late 70s. This ultimately favoured violence and expulsion as the most desirable means of protecting a mythologized English identity and culture.

Nevertheless, whether the BFS manages to disentangle herself from the webs of contradictory meanings surrounding English identity in the song seems questionable. 'Oh England, My Lionheart' shows how the BFS is bound up with the nostalgia of her cultural context: How she perpetuates mythologies of Englishness that have, in different political contexts and enunciations, grave social consequences.

Whether the BFS is 'aware' of such implications, or if she wants to extricate herself from these structures and myths also seems questionable. Certainly her expressions in the song embody an intensely romantic yearning for idealised representations of England's bygone years. The absence of aggression *towards* other cultures or peoples who want to come and share the glory of living in England's 'garden' suggest that she was not interested in promoting the racist ideas that were popular at the time. The BFS places nationalism in the context of love and loyalty.

Whatever the ethical difficulties the song presents, the BFS provided very little opposition to the status quo as she developed her presentation as England's good and obedient daughter. The BFS is certainly a queer radical in terms of her exploration of gender and sexuality. In the context of national and cultural identity, she presents more reactionary tendencies. Later in her life the BFS will wrestle with the structures of guilt, complicity and implication this early identification with Englishness produces. She begins to gain a historical awareness of her position as a white woman from a nation with a continuing history of violent colonial policies. We will see this worked out on *The Dreaming*. In 1978 at least, the BFS remained grounded in the roots of the English garden.

The homoerotic Orientalism of the BFS

Claiming an English identity has concrete implications for how the BFS can speak about ethnic and cultural difference. Through becoming English she situates herself within legacies of colonialism and racism. On *Lionheart* and *Never For Ever* the BFS uses Orientalist devices. Orientalism is the cultural expression of western imperialism. It manifests in appropriation of, and the projection of, fantasies about Eastern cultures. Its titillation should not disguise its violence. Many of these fantasies are sexualised. As the BFS is a perverse creature, Orientalist motifs appear as she explores her own and others' sexualities.

Since the Eighteenth century Western writers have projected stereotypical fantasies of exotic otherness onto the East or the Orient. In this construction 'the East' is feminised and represented as a space to explore sexualities and all things wanton. It is a safe space for Westerners to enjoy sexuality away from the equally constructed, rational West. This is also true for the BFS. Orientalism is used as a way that she can talk about sexuality. In her female body in the late 1970s, the BFS was not free to discuss sex in the way she would like. Orientalist tropes provide an outlet for her insatiable desire.

We should remember that the BFS of *Lionheart* is a queer beast. Her femininity, most of the time on the album, is a kind of effeminised masculinity. This is linked to male homosexuality. The BFS's Orientalism draws upon this aspect of her subjectivity. When she feminises the Orient, she does so in a very male homoerotic way. Her sexualised fantasies do not feminise oriental women. They feminise oriental men. In so doing, the BFS's fantasies effeminise the Orient itself. The BFS is implicated with the homoerotics of colonialism.

What is Orientalism?

Orientalism is a body of Western knowledge about cultural difference and otherness. It is a concept first developed in the work of Edward Said. He published *Orientalism* in 1978. Many other writers have since contributed to the debate.[38] Orientalism provided a critical language to discuss how Western imperialist representations of 'the East' dehumanize and homogenise vastly difference cultures. They do this by creating stereotypes that present 'the East' as hyper-sexualised, exotic, despotic, irrational and heathen. In short everything that the West supposedly is not. Orientalism works by instating a binary opposition between West/ East. This is used to affirm the cultural superiority of western cultures. In doing so, it was used as a justification for colonial ventures. Orientalism '"created [a] body of theory and practice," designed, consciously or unconsciously, to serve the interests of the European imperial powers.'[39]

Orientalist representations became part of the dominant fabric of Western culture in the nineteenth century. This was a time when Britain was undergoing huge industrial expansion and engaging in unprecedented imperial activity. Stuart Schaar summarises:

> By the nineteenth century, Orientalist discourse had become set, and its stereotypes disseminated throughout western culture: Orientalists had developed a consensus. Since this consensus was congruent with the interests of those in power, Orientalist ideas freely permeated aesthetic, economic, historical and political texts. Orientalism became an integral part of western culture.[40]

Orientalism came to be crucial in this period in defining the West's ideas about itself. The West came to know itself as self-contained, rational, familiar, moral, just and Christian in contrast to the irrational, exotic, erotic, despotic and heathen Orient.

Lionheart and *Never For Ever* abound with Orientalist stereotypes. There are decadent and monstrous appetites ('Coffee Homeground'), effeminacy (the whole of *Lionheart* is delivered in a high camp, falsetto style), mystery and sexuality. Sexuality is part of the irresistible mystery of the Orient. It is continually 'associated with sexual promise'[41] and fecundity.

The BFS recycles many Orientalist tropes. They are part of the culture she grew up in. As mentioned earlier, context matters. It affects what we can say and how we can say it. While dehumanising representations of the Orient certainly should be deconstructed, it is not hard to see their appeal to the BFS. She uses Orientalist tropes as an available cultural space to talk about sex and sexuality. As a recently self-defined English girl, these sorts of devices were only available by displacing those desires elsewhere, away from woman and away from the West.

A clear example of an Orientalist strategy on *Lionheart* can be found in the song 'Kashka from Baghdad.' The song is about a male homosexual couple. As the title suggests, the drama revolves around the especially interesting life of the protagonist, Kashka. Kashka's cultural and ethnic origins are highlighted in the title. He is 'from Baghdad.' This implies that these characteristics are enough for a white, Western audience to already form expectations about his character. The other song titles on the album often have a metaphorical quality to them. The use of such a title suggests that the name 'Kashka from Baghdad' conjures and prompts enough images and ideas to serve as a metaphor in itself. We imagine that the general atmosphere of the song would be moody, sensual and despotic, as well as many other culturally constructed clichés.

As a textual and thematic device on 'Kashka from Baghdad,' Orientalism is used to invoke scandalous sexually deviant behaviour. This forms the dramatic attraction of the song. Paddy Bush describes the song as 'a number with an Islamic flavour to it.' It uses an instrument called a *strumento da porco* that '*sounds* like a santour which is a traditional Arabian instrument played with hammers.'[42] Paddy Bush comments that the *strumento da porco sounds like* a traditional Arabian instrument. He demonstrates the instances of appropriation that is a common feature of Western musical practices. As Scott comments, 'when Orientalism appropriates music from another culture it is not used simply to represent the Other; it is used to represent our own thoughts about the Other.'[43] To be more playful, the use of an instrument that sounds like a sound is another example of how artifice runs through the album.

The musical accompaniment to and arrangement of 'Kashka from Baghdad' - the orchestration, delivery of the main vocal line, and extra vocals – reveal the BFS's attempt at creating an Orientalised atmosphere. The song is shrouded in themes of mystery and voyeurism. It remains persistently joyful. The music is insistent and brooding. The build-up of deep male voices form the backdrop to the chorus. They suggest sinister movements of bodies as they pass through the dark night. These voices also form the end of the song, as the chant 'Ut-cha ev'ry night/ Don't you know they're seen/ won't you let me laugh/ let me in your love' (*LH*) is repeated to fade.

The use of voices in this way, and the shivering, percussive chimes that rattle from the beginning, create an ambience of unfamiliarity and suspicion. Experimenting and exploring the unfamiliar is often the fate of the BFS. However there is a certain element of estrangement from the cultural landscape evoked in 'Kashka from Baghdad.' There is also yearning and attachment. For example, the lyrics in the second chorus state: 'I long to be with them' (*LH*). The singer feels an attraction towards Kashka and his friend because of the 'music from Kashka's house' (*LH*). This can be heard from the street outside.

The sinister atmosphere of the song does not arise from the Orient's mysterious nature alone. The song is all about watching people's behaviour. Really it's an expression of simple nosiness. If the deep build-up of voices evokes a dark street, it is because the speaker of the song is positioned standing on the street. From there s/he expresses judgement and speculates about the lives of the two men who live in a sinful way. 'Kashka from Baghdad' is nothing more than glorified neighbourhood gossip about male homosexuality. However it is not a condemnation of homosexuality. There is empathy and fascination expressed through the music. Nevertheless the song does partake in exploiting the scandalous aspect of homosexuality to create its dramatic effect.

Lionheart is a very homosensual album. Male homosexuality still remains discussed in protective arenas. Let us not forget that male homosexuality only became legal in Britain in 1968. 'Wow' is partly inspired by gay men in show business and the theatre. Homosexuals are safe to exist in showbiz, because that is not everyday life. In 'Kashka from Baghdad' the homosexual 'sin' is interrogated, watched and imagined at a site far away from England. It is a suitably safe place, where male homoerotic action can be explored without tainting the polite contours of British society. As Joseph Boone suggests:

> The geopolitical realities of the Arabic Orient become a psychic screen on which to project psychic fantasies of illicit sexuality and unbridled excess – including as Malek Alloua has observed, 'generalized perversion' and, as Edward Said puts it, 'sexual experience unobtainable in Europe,' that is, 'a different type of sexuality.'[44]

Boone's comment was made in the context of Western writers travelling to the Arabic Orient to experience 'the different types of sexuality' that apparently, were not available in Europe. It provides a useful way to think about how the BFS uses the geopolitical *fantasy* of the Arabic Orient in order to talk about homosexuality.

The use of the Orient in this way does maintain the idea that homosexuality is *not* something that happens in England. However, the song also betrays the cultural shame that British culture directed towards gay men. 'Kashka from Baghdad lives in sin they say,/ With another man,/ But no-one knows who' (*LH*).

The sinfulness of living with another man is immediately highlighted at the beginning of the song: 'Old friends never call there,/ Some wonder if there's life inside at all,/ If there's life inside at all (*LH*). This creates a context whereby Kashka and his faceless partner's actions will be subject to judgement and surveillance by the community that surrounds them. They do not speak for themselves: *the community* says that they live in 'sin.' 'We know the lady who rents the room,/ She catches them calling a la lune' (*LH*). The culturally invisible, 'only behind closed doors' and 'undisclosed identity' of male homosexual life is commented on. There is the inclusion of the anonymous man with whom he shares his life: 'no-one knows who' this is.

Clearly Kashka has turned his back on conventional society. He has lost his friends. They 'never call there.' Some wonder if he is now dead because of his scandalous lifestyle. The association of homosexuality with metaphorical death is consistent with patriarchal conceptions of masculinity. For men, being penetrated is similar to dying, Leo Bersani has argued in his article 'Is the Rectum a Grave?'[45] Penetration signals a breakdown of psychical, sexual and bodily boundaries. These would usually remain secure and distinct. At the start of Bush's song, Kashka is *as good as dead* by the standards of those around him. Is there any 'life inside at all' now he treads the path of sexual deviance?

At the end of the opening verse we return to the perspectives of the community that surrounds the two men. They provide more details about their situation: '*We know* the lady who rents the room/ *Who catches them* calling a la lune' (*LH*, italics mine). In this verse there is a concentrated sense of surveillance combined with neighbourhood reports. 'We know' a lady who will tell us, for it is she who 'catches them' doing what they are doing. The displaced despotisms of British culture are disguised by dressing up Western bigotry with Oriental signifiers. What is essentially 'curtain twitching' becomes, in the frame of the story of 'Kashka from Baghdad,' something seemingly more exciting.

The chorus interrupts the trend in the song. It offers a celebratory intervention using major, uplifting chords: '*At night they're seen*/ Laughing, loving,/ They know the way/ To be happy (*LH*, italics mine).

Still there is the idea of the spectral or vampiric homosexual, as the couple's behaviour is glimpsed at night, *and only at night*. There is the stress, in the first line of the chorus, on how the BFS – who comes to embody the spying, fascinated community – captures the men in his/her gaze. The chorus does strongly introduce the idea of their love and happiness. This is communicated through the lyrics and in the way that each line of the chorus is punctuated by drums before the final strain of 'happy' is stretched into the second verse. This sets the lyrical tone for the rest of the song.

The second verse confesses that 'They never go for walks' (*LH*) with the coy explanation that 'Maybe it's because the moon's not bright enough' (*LH*). The moon's illumination is not enough to shine light upon their behaviour. Despite the continuing obsessive atmosphere of surveillance that characterises the song, the next few lines do depict a shift in emphasis. The song comes to focus on the love and mystery of the two men's relationship. The next lines display a strong desire and identification with them: 'There's light in love you see./ *I watch their shadows*' and later, '*I long to be with them*' (*LH*, italics mine). The odd behaviour of these two men, 'tall and slim in the window opposite,' is justified by the illuminating quality of their love. They can still only be seen through, or as, shadows. The BFS partially distances herself from the community's disdain. S/he 'long[s] to be with them' (*LH*). These lines provide a conflict and tension within the song, providing an internal challenge to the judgement of the community. The BFS partially splits away from it. The attraction of Kashka's house is that 'you can hear music' (*LH*) coming from it. Presumably the BFS wishes that they could participate in the music-making. 'Music' here is a coy metaphor for sex.

'Kashka from Baghdad' describes the BFS's fantasy to partake in group sex. S/he gazes obsessively and longingly through the curtains of Kashka's house, impelled by curiosity. The song displays a desire to indulge in a 'different' kind of sexuality. A sexuality far outside of the prescribed options available to women in a hetero-normative, patriarchal culture. This exists both at a literal level and a fantastical one. The BFS's use of Orientalism here is comparable to many other Western writers who utilise the geopolitical arena of the Arabic Orient in the way Boone describes above. They use it to psychically explore desires that are essentially unspeakable and can only be acknowledged through the shadows and veils of secrecy.

The BFS's gender and sexuality are powerfully transformed through her gay voyeurism. This use of a queer strategy allows for her a greater fluidity of desire and identification. Fantasy and sexuality are potent combinations for the BFS. The important point is that Orientalism allows her to stray into such unexplored arenas.

'Kashka from Baghdad' sees the BFS use Orientalist stereotypes in order to explore sexualities and mobile spaces of desire that would not be accessible or possible within a model of hetero-normative, patriarchal femininity. As she does this she reinforces Orientalist clichés about the exotic and highly sexualised arena of the East. Orientalism is used as a way to articulate and deviate from prescribed gender and sexual roles.

Chapter Two has seen the BFS grow away from her first incarnation on *The Kick Inside*. She needed to do it and find other ways of being. In *Lionheart* she undergoes a number of queer transformations. She does this in order to negotiate the limitations of her female sexed body. She draws upon camp in 'Hammer Horror' and 'Coffee Homeground,' queer temporalities in 'In Search of Peter Pan' and the theatre in 'Wow' in order to do so. The BFS also positions herself within hegemonic and essentialised notions of English identity.

The BFS is a perverse creature and uses Orientalist strategies in order to satisfy her fascination for sexuality. However, this means she reinforces representational stereotypes of 'exotic' Eastern 'otherness.' This occurs most notably in 'Kashka from Baghdad.' In the next stage of the BFS's life she enjoys an interlude as we briefly consider the next album she produced, *Never for Ever.* This interlude will ease her passage from her queer life on *Lionheart* to her different manifestation on 1982's album *The Dreaming*.

The BFS changes, yet again. This time it's serious.

Never for Ever: the continuity and change of the BFS

Never for Ever is a point of transition for the BFS. Within it she explores many of the themes that were important in her early life, as well as beginning an important shift which we will see played out on *The Dreaming*. While the BFS is a transformative creature she is also consistent. She likes to develop ideas that stretch the full spectrum of her imagination and she remains embedded in familiar behaviour.

Never for Ever is marked by the same queer fascinations with taboo sexuality of *The Kick Inside* and *Lionheart*. For example, 'The Infant's Kiss' is inspired by the 1961 film *The Innocents*, which dramatises a governesses' obsession with the children she looks after, in particular the young boy Miles who is possessed by the spirit of an adult man: 'There's a man behind those eyes.'[1] The BFS performs as the governess to tell a tale of spiritual and emotional obsession, 'I want to smack but I hold back/ I only want to touch' (*NFE*) while the simple orchestration and violin riffs convey the tense, creeping horror of the film.

'The Infant's Kiss' again shows how the BFS uses cultural texts as inspiration for her own. Through this strategy she infuses popular culture with perverse stories which have their origin in supposed 'high culture' (*The Innocents* itself was based on Henry James' *The Turn of the Screw*). In doing so, she re-makes the possibility of the popular song, using it to re-interpret stories and putting her unique twist on them.

Never For Ever also contains another example of homoerotic Orientalism. This occurs on the song 'Egypt.' The song uses the same instrument that is used to evoke an 'Islamic flavour' in 'Kashka from Baghdad,' the *strumento de porco*. Egypt occupies a special place in the Western imagination. Joseph Boone argues that it exists as an:

> intermediate zone, 'a foothold, a staging point,' that signifies liminality and indeterminacy itself. As the realm of nonfixity, moreover, it has become a ready made symbol for that interior world of the polymorphous perverse that its western visitors find uncannily familiar, and, as an effect of repression, unimaginably estranging.[2]

Many of these qualities can be found on the song 'Egypt.' The country's imagined terrains and buildings are draped in sexualised imagery and are suggestive of penetration. 'Follow up the Nile, Deep to much deeper,' (*NFE*) and 'the pyramids sound lonely tonight' (*NFE*) while 'their symmetry *gets right inside of me*' (*NFE*, italics mine).

The sense of sexual and romantic discomfort is alluded to in the lines 'I'm busy chasing up my demon' (*NFE*). This suggests there is something 'unspeakable' or 'demonic' about the desire that the BFS goes to explore in Egypt. The feeling of uneasiness and paranoia is compounded at the end of the song. This features a series of desperate screams that echo outwards and then feed into a dramatic build-up of chants and heavy tom drums. The song merges back into the anguished scream, suggesting all the horror of repressed desire.

In keeping with the tradition of Orientalist representations, 'Egypt' as a fantasised region is feminised. As I explained in the previous chapter, this does not necessarily mean that it is always a woman who is the object of desire. In the queer world of the BFS, masculinity does not automatically 'belong' to men, nor does femininity automatically 'belong' to women. The second verse of the song dramatises the intoxicating aspects of the land, rooted in its overpowering sexuality: 'My Pussy Queen, knows all my secrets,/ I'll never fall in love again' (*NFE*). The land offers the BFS 'Egyptian Delights' while 'She's got me with that feline 'guise,/ Got me in those desert eyes,/ Oh, I'm in love with Egypt' (*NFE*).

The second verse contains many clichéd Orientalist representations.

The BFS mentions the 'Egyptian Delights.' The seduction is completed as the BFS 'drift[s] with dunes./ I whisper of the tombs' (*NFE*), conjuring sensuality. The BFS's position in terms of gender in this song is, again, very interesting. The BFS is positioned in a structurally masculine space, even as her gender in the song is not made explicit. This creates space for gendered speculation. It is in line with the queer tendencies of the BFS and her ability to shift gendered space.

The song describes desire for the feminine – 'Egypt' as a space on which to project fantasy and desire – and for the 'Pussy Queen' who knows all my secrets.' The 'Pussy Queen' may also refer to Sekhmet, the Egyptian goddess who is usually portrayed as a woman with a head of a lioness. Her name means 'she who is powerful.' This is consistent with the BFS's interest in constructing counter-mythologies grounded in the feminine.

'Egypt' sees the BFS again recycle Orientalist tropes. By doing so she creates multiple gendered and desiring spaces that move within the song. In 'Egypt' the BFS leans towards a queer understanding of desire. The indeterminacy and liminality of Egypt as an imagined space allows her to do this. In the first verse, the images of penetration can suggest vaginal penetration, but could equally imply anal penetration. This allows the BFS to both desire and objectify like a Western male sexual tourist. Anal penetration and sodomy have been culturally taboo in Western culture, particularly since the Enlightenment. The ambience of repression, secrecy and destructive desire that the song hints at lyrically and musically suggests that this is more likely to be the type of penetration that the song sings of.

Equally, if we accept that the BFS presents herself as female, the song can be read as describing female homosexual and homoerotic desire communicated through goddess worship. In either sense, 'Egypt' radically departs from a hetero-normative model of desire. However it does this through reactively reinforcing Western Orientalist stereotypes about Egypt as a space of polymorphous perversity.

Another example of the female homoeroticism of the BFS can be found in the video to the single from the album, 'Babooshka.' While the song itself is presented in a heterosexual 'frame' (the story of a wife wanting to win back the loyalties of her husband and inject a bit of sauciness into their relationship), the video itself plays right into the hands of some of the best lesbian camp ever depicted on film.

In the video the BFS shifts between two identities. The veiled woman dressed all in black mourning her waning relationship and a voraciously sexual, sword yielding, phallic woman. The latter character is adorned in an outfit that Xena, Warrior Princess would envy – a tight fitting chainmail bra, green bikini bottom, gold straps that wrap around the top of her thighs, all topped off with a high femme gold and green scarf that glistens in the bursts of light that mark the change between the scenes. The upper half of the BFS's body looks muscular and powerful, her sexiness exuding from her formidable strength.

This is an expression of sexuality that moves far beyond heterosexual convention, as the BFS parades her phallic symbol in parodic and threatening ways. As her sword cuts through air, she slices through conventional formations of gender and sexuality and opens up new possible desiring realities, for the video produces visual codes completely at odds with the actual narrative of the song. It creates a visibility for the integration of butch-femme high camp before it was known to exist.

The word 'Babooshka' itself, the Russian word meaning 'Grandma,' although having a pleasant alliterative effect, only serves to conjure the kind of dowdy sexuality that has been the hallmark of lesbianism throughout history (and which, of course, is incredibly sexy).[3] As we said in the previous chapter, the BFS is very queer indeed and this only proves the point further.

Never for Ever as transition

While *Never for Ever* looks back to the early tendencies of the BFS's life, it also looks forward. It is an important transition point to the emerging forms of life that will appear on *The Dreaming*, an album which we will consider in depth. This transformation occurs to the BFS's voice - it becomes politicised and more engaged with the world. To understand this further, we will consider the video for the anti-nuclear protest song 'Breathing.'

As I have said before, the BFS is very much of her time. Her interest in promoting anti-nuclear protest was part of early 1980s political culture. At that time the threat of nuclear war was very real in the public consciousness as Britain was still in the midst of the Cold War. The government fuelled public fears about nuclear devastation with its 'Protect and Survive' campaign which distributed booklets to all the homes in Britain, advising them what to do in the event of a nuclear attack. Sasha Roseneil describes its impact:

> The booklets distributed by the state as part of this campaign advised, in the event of a nuclear attack, whitewashing the windows of one's house and hiding under a door propped against a wall with a substantial supply of food and a transistor radio. The effect of such public information was to increase public awareness of preparation for a nuclear war in Europe.[4]

The 'Protect and Survive' campaign led to strong resistance to nuclear weapons in the early 1980s. There were many protests, most notably Greenham Women's Peace Camp, which lasted from the early 1980s to the early 1990s. Greenham created a political space where women mobilised a caring, emotional and nurturing politics to challenge ideologies of violence and war. This aimed to counteract of the destructiveness of patriarchal cultures with its fixation on ever innovative modes of devastation.

This kind of alternative political voice is what the BFS mobilises in 'Breathing.' The video itself offers a creative exploration of the process of how women's voices *become* political. This is presented as a movement out of the womb and into the political.

The video for 'Breathing' sees the BFS recover a relationship with a mother figure. The video begins with the BFS inside a large womb, complete with umbilical cord. There she moves minimally for the duration of the first verse and she speaks from inside the maternal body. The song describes the permeability of that body which breaks down rigid distinctions between objects: 'Outside gets inside,/ *Through her skin*' (*NFE*, italics mine).

The womb is a place of refuge from the volatile landscape outside. This has just suffered a nuclear explosion: 'Last night in the sky,/ Such a bright light' (*NFE*). The maternal body is called upon as a source of life support. It nurtures basic instincts, like breathing: 'Breathing my mother in,/ Breathing, my beloved in,/ Breathing, Breathing her nicotine, breathing,/ Breathing the fall out-in, out-in, out-in, out in, out-in' (*NFE*).

The BFS moves her hand against the womb in a similar way to a baby kicking. The lyrics – 'out-in, out-in' - mimic the action of being born. The relationship with the mother in the song is also figured as a romantic one. She is referred to as 'beloved.' She calls upon the relationship with the mother in order to nurture the emergence of an uncompromised female-identified political language. She uses the mother to support her political desires.

After the second chorus the BFS is seen tumbling out of the womb into a soundscape populated by voices and noises mimicking the wind. There are radio transmissions, a fading in-and-out chorus of male voices, fretless bass guitar and minimal percussion. These serve to create an atmosphere of nuclear devastation. The climax to the song is approached where drums and a driving electric guitar riff kick in, marking the beginning of the dramatic outro. This is the space where a private language, nurtured by the breath of the mother, becomes political.

As Irigaray asserts, 'breathing itself incites to an awakening.'[5] In the video, the shift between the womb and the world is made by pulling apart two suns. A blast of atomic light illuminates the BFS and a group of male companions upon a hillside. A fierce wind blows over them. The camera moves to the group wading through the water – another important female symbol – whilst the BFS and the people, dressed in all-white nuclear-resistant power suits, sing: 'What are we going to do without/ Ooh, please, let me breathe' (*NFE*). Later they demand 'Leave us something to breathe,/ Ooh, Life is –/ Breathing' (*NFE*).

The vocal delivery is dramatic, emotional and aggressively moving. It demands an emotional response to her pleas. The BFS's vocal tactic is transformed when she moves outside of the womb. Her speech opens up to embrace everybody. She abandons the calm approach presented in the first section of the song. In doing so she presents a politically affective, public, feminine language.

This song and its video mark a point of connection between the early life of the BFS and her life that is to come on *The Dreaming*. In her earlier life the BFS is concerned to celebrate feminine culture and symbols. She draws upon the potency of the maternal body and what it can generate. On *The Dreaming* the BFS adopts a politicised, aggressive voice that emerges on the finale to 'Breathing.' It is the emergence of this voice which colours the next stage of the BFS's journey. It is the promise that the BFS, yet again, changes into forms as you have never seen her before.

The Dreaming, the Breakdown and Becomings of the BFS

1982's *The Dreaming* sees another dramatic shift in the life of the BFS; you'd almost not recognise her from before. *The Dreaming* is the BFS mad, bad and angry. Gone are the sweet and cooing, charming good English girl of *Lionheart* and the melodious heroine of *The Kick Inside*. On *The Dreaming* the BFS shouts and screams. She is traumatised. She rips her whole world apart but only to put it together again. She has a breakdown - in fact she has several.

As violent, angry and scary as these experiences are for her on the album, the breakdowns are also breakthroughs into new ways of being. They are created through encounters with machines, animals and other forms of cultural difference. These help reconstruct the new life of the BFS.

This chapter will delve into the further transformations of the BFS as she radically shifts away from her previous selves. To understand these shifts we need to introduce a different critical language because the changes that occur on *The Dreaming* are incredibly vast. The tools that we use to read these changes need to address this.

The transformations of BFS on *The Dreaming* happen through a series of breakdowns and becomings. Becoming is an idea developed by French post-structuralists Gilles Deleuze and Felix Guattari. It can be found in their book *A Thousand Plateaus*, which was first published in French in 1980. Becoming is a way of understanding how subjectivities are created and is another key to unlock the multiplicity of the BFS.

Becomings emphasise how our subjectivities are made with each other. That is, in a space where people, animals, plants, trees or machines meet and recombine in an *encounter*. In the words of physicist Karen Barad, becoming is where subjectivities 'emerge through, their intra-action...[and] *mutual entanglement*.'[1] Becoming allows us to understand how subjectivities can influence each other to create new forms of life.

Becomings are also understood as post-human. That is, they embrace the relationship between human and non or un-human entities. The non-human is a wide category embracing everything that exists that isn't human. Post-human perspectives challenge anthropocentrism – the idea that the human is the centre of the universe and the only life form that matters. From a post-human viewpoint *everything* has life. Or, in theoretical terms, everything has agency. This agency can have an impact upon the world. No matter how big or small, this impact carries significance.

In a traditional humanist standpoint, it is only the human that has a right to this life or agency. Man is an island who is superior to all that surrounds him. He is the subject while everything else is an object. This was the ontology or mode of being that the BFS was previously most easily identified with, although she had made significant strides on *The Kick Inside* to celebrate female sexual difference which challenges this framework. Humanism denies the ways in which subjectivities are *created together* through interaction and mutual becoming. It is an alienated model of being.

Before the mention of post-humanism conjures robots, the space age and freakish monsters in your mind, it is important to understand the everyday ways we are post-human. When humans first used a spoon to eat food, they encountered an object that transformed what they could do. Ever since a human stroked a cat and felt good, they have been post-human because they have been transformed through an encounter with an animal. They have felt love through purring, non-human life. These types of everyday encounters expand horizons and alter our subjectivities forever. In them, both human and non-human become something more than what they were. This is the crux of becoming.

Producing the new forms of BFS

On *The Dreaming* the BFS gains control of a new tool that furthers her multiplicity: the recording studio. The album was the first one that the BFS completely produced herself and she would do so for every release that followed it. The difference this complete control allowed her is evident upon listening. The album draws upon experimental production techniques which feed into the alternative ways the BFS presents herself to the listening public. We now find her writhing with machines, as well as her emotions.

The becoming machine of *The Dreaming* is realised literally through the BFS's use of studio technology. Here the studio is used not only to translate musical ideas by recording them; it is a compositional tool in itself. Through exploring this relationship with studio technology, the BFS is expanded in the process. On the album, production is emphasised as much as the vocal lines or instruments. This allows us to experience the record as a work of process. That is, we are conscious of it is as a constructed piece of work. We are not simply left with a smooth product we can *easily* consume. *The Dreaming* combines flesh, noise, machine, melody and language with rough, noisy edges.

The Dreaming invites listeners to consider it as a construction of parts working together. Sometimes they work against one another. The album is about synthesis *and* collision. The masses of vocal and instrumental layers construct not simply a collection of songs. They create a 'veritable *machinic* opera tying together orders, species and heterogeneous qualities.'[2] The music is grandiose, ambitious and hyperbolic. It unites different entities together in surprising and creative ways. Things you wouldn't expect to fit together actually do.

The Dreaming still remains a disorientating affair. Its sonic fibres stick out and poke at the listener. Its boundary-pushing and experimental rhythms encourage participation in a constant state of disorientation. To understand and love it properly, we need to lose our sense of what the BFS was up to that point, and be aware that we all have the right to change.

This disorientation partly emerges from multiple forms of other/ed voices, rhythms, stories and bodies that live on the album. *The Dreaming* differs from the Orientalist strategies on *Lionheart* and *Never for Ever*. It attempts to move away from stereotypical Western representations of non-Western and indigenous cultures. I will explain how this strategy is not completely successful; the BFS remains implicated in racialised power structures, even if she tries to find new ways of dismantling them.

At the very least, she can be seen to undo and question the taken for granted Western cultural imperialism that flourishes on *Lionheart*. On *The Dreaming* there is a fuller identification with the BFS's *own otherness* as a woman. This occurs at the same time as she moves away from the exclusive English identity that influences her early life on *The Kick Inside*, *Lionheart* and *Never for Ever*. The BFS is also activated by an awareness of the violent historical realities of colonialism. This provides *The Dreaming* with the fuller sense of accountability that is arguably lacking in other albums.

Finally, *The Dreaming* sees the BFS experiment with different storytelling strategies. She does not merely represent events and characters. On *The Dreaming* there is often no single narrator telling stories. There is a more regular use of the 'I' but this 'I' is never unified. It is always multiple and in a constant state of change from song to song, even within the song.

Instead of story-telling at a basic level, the BFS inhabits the characters' spatial, sensory and historical imaginations. This enables her to become more fully immersed in a character, situation, their feeling and sensations. She undergoes a shift from *describing* stories to *becoming* them. This of course was a quality of her early life ('Wuthering Heights', and 'The Infant's Kiss,' for example), but it is on *The Dreaming* that this strategy is most fully explored.

Breakdown 1.
The breakdown of the BFS is the breakdown of everything

The Dreaming is about the deconstruction of certainties. It witnesses the breakdown of the BFS. The album should be understood in the context of post-punk music that was its contemporary in the late 1970s and early 1980s. Artists working in this genre were, according to Simon Reynolds, 'totally confident that there were still places to go with rock [and there was] a whole new future to invent,' believing that 'radical content demands radical form.'[3]

The experimental aesthetics of post-punk provided a musical space where the BFS could explore a number of different musical, vocal and production styles. Boundary-pushing vocal performances, the use of synthesizers and tribal drumming also connect *The Dreaming* with this lineage. Post-punk's influence is found in how *The Dreaming* rearranges and pulls apart traditional song structures. This undermines traditional notions of mastery and control which are normatively used to measure 'good' song writing. Much of the work is not recognisable as standard pop songs. Many thought the BFS lost it or had gone too far. To this day, the album receives polarised reviews that either affirm its genius or dismiss it as nonsense.

Listening to 'Sat in Your Lap,' the first song and single from the album, you might think the BFS *had* gone too far. It is a drum-led, synthesizer feast; a manic-depressive riot through linguistic, sonic and structural breakdowns. The experience of listening to this song provides its audience with the one certainty of the album: that the world of BFS is falling radically apart. The chorus is a hymn to the pursuit of fleeting knowledge: 'Some say that knowledge is something that you never have/ Some say that knowledge is something sat in your lap' (*TD*).[4]

The guttural repeated 'Ooohs' after the '(I just begin)' create the effect of physical punches. These place the BFS amidst a cataclysmic breakdown. The song provides no space to recover. The BFS is thrust back into the milieu of torrential self-doubt, heightened by intense emotions. The situation gets more exaggerated as the song moves towards its finale.

Musically 'Sat in Your Lap' is epic in proportions, tempestuous in fact. It has more in common with a Shakespearean tragedy than a pop song. The BFS parodies the colloquialisms of the Shakespearean period, 'My cup she never overfloweth and 'tis I that moan and groaneth' (*TD*). This also rewrites the biblical language of the 23rd psalm: 'My Cup Overfloweth.'

'Sat in Your in Your Lap' has unforgettable hallmarks. There is a drum line that drives throughout and a synthesizer that rises like a threatening, portentous storm. The repeated 'oohs' convey a sense of continual and deep frustration. Underneath these most distinguishable expressions of histrionic despair are layers of piano and bass. These never rise outwards like the other elements. On top of this the BFS's trademark voices are imposed. They are used to create many perspectives within the song and are an example of her multiplicity. These different voices inflict the violence that pulls the BFS down from her previous position of certainty.

'Sat in Your Lap' does not remain merely an exploration of *personal* frustration, even if it displays a deconstruction of the knowing self. The song is a comment on the inevitable breakdown that occurs when people attempt to apply reason too strictly. It challenges the idea that intellectual knowledge and balance can be accessed via the mind alone. This is an idea that has structured centuries of Western thought, a tradition dominated by the Cartesian subject.

Descartes's Cartesian subject is based on a mind/body split. He is conjured by the famous phrase, 'I think therefore I am.' The influence of Cartesian ideas in culture can be seen by the fact that this is one of the few philosophical statements that many people intuitively know off by heart. It is common sense knowledge in culture. We know it without realising we do.

'Sat in Your Lap' on the other hand, dramatically challenges this statement. It does this by asking whether rational thinking is *possible* or even *desirable*. It's more like 'I can't think therefore I am.' It asks whether there can be balance within a culture that believes the intellect is the only means through which to understand the world.

'Sat in Your Lap' dramatises the collapse of the Cartesian subject of knowledge and reason and the BFS is embroiled within this fight. It presents the limitations of intellectual reason. 'Some say that heaven is hell, some say that hell is heaven' (*TD*).

The focus on intellectual ways of understanding - 'I want to be a lawyer, I want to be a scholar' is presented as worthless: 'In my dome of ivory, a home of activity... I hold a cup of wisdom, but there is nothing within' (*TD*). This futility is reflected in the music. The disjointed stuttering of drums, hysterical layers of synthesizers and high-pitched vocals wail about the impossibility of knowledge. It suggests there is a fundamental *un-productivity* when too much emphasis is placed upon the mind in order to understand matter(s).

The breakdown of knowledge that is dramatised in the song also has racial dimensions. This becomes apparent when considering the promotional video. In it the BFS adorns herself in a white dress and large pointed hat carrying the letter 'D.' Since the seventeenth century the hat has come to symbolise a dunce, a kind of intellectual slang for a person who is incapable of learning. The whiteness of the BFS's clothes and hat implies a connection between whiteness and stupidity.

As the BFS attempts to dance to the song's asymmetrical rhythms, phantom like white figures flash by either side of her head. As the verse merges to the pre-chorus, the figures become embodied and roller-skate across the floor. They are dressed with pointed white hats, robes and masks. These evoke the costumes that members of the Ku Klux Klan, the white supremacist group based in America responsible for racial lynching, wear. These figures follow the BFS throughout the video like a ghostly entourage.

The appearance of three black bodies adorned with a Minotaur heads reinforces the stereotypical racialisation of bodies in the video. As black is played against white it makes the black body appear animalistic and frightening. In histories of colonialism and slavery, black people have often been portrayed as closer to animals. This has been used as an excuse for white people to violently exploit black people, based on the idea that they are more intelligent and therefore somehow have the right to. The dominance of white over black is seen as the roller-skating Minotaur acts as the BFS's slave, carrying the white dunce on his back.

Highlighting these racial dynamics is not necessarily the intention of the BFS in the video. She may not be conscious of her racism or her desire to deconstruct it. Nevertheless, it can't be avoided that the presence of all the figures in the video, collectively serve to evoke racialised stereotypes and their inherent power relations. The way they appear together suggests these power relations are cracking up, as the BFS breaks apart too, under this pressure.

The video for 'Sat in Your Lap' lays bare white supremacist racialised cultural codes. It is limited in that it implies critique rather than stating it, even if it does create space for reflection on the stupidity of whiteness. This is the stupidity that throughout history has used ideas about being civilised and rational to justify slavery, genocide and colonialism. In the video the BFS uses colour to bring the 'black and white' logics of the song to the surface and asks the people watching it to make the connections. It suggests that knowledge and power are encased within racialised frameworks as much as they are within gendered ones.

As 'Sat in your Lap' reaches its conclusion it moves towards non-Western cultures as an avenue to escape the limitations of Western knowledge and value systems. The ending of the song charts the speaker's planned escape across a terrain of elements, providing a suitably hyperbolic exit to the tortuous landscapes of the song: 'Some grey and white matter, (Give me the Karma Mama/ a jet to Mecca, Tibet or Jeddah,/ To Salisbury' (*TD*). It is the promise of 'the longest journey, across the desert,/ Across the weather, across the elements,/ Across the water)' (*TD*).

In this final section the BFS pleads for escape into more flexible spaces from which she can learn in the 'grey and white matter.' Western and non-Western systems are drawn upon in the desperate search for a calm space that moves *across* ideas.

The breakdowns that occur on this album do not merely signal the end of the BFS's capacity to know, learn and understand matters. Quite the contrary. 'Sat in Your Lap' is an attempt to exit from Cartesian, masculine and white supremacist systems of knowledge and structure. It is a crucial site of departure for the BFS. The rest of the album will move on from it. Importantly 'Sat in Your Lap' is placed at the beginning of *The Dreaming* and subsequent songs fall into the deconstructive space that it clears.

'Sat in Your Lap' displays an aggressive vulnerability. Politically it provides a space where feminine experiences of authoritarian, patriarchal knowledge systems can be expressed. The song revels in the BFS's *incapacity* to understand and apply herself in a conscientious manner. It challenges the performance of confidence, rationality and mastery which is usually synonymous with scholarly learning and examination.

'Sat in Your Lap' radically highlights the limits of these systems and the incapacity of the Cartesian subject to *know* anything at all: 'knowledge is ho ho ho' (*TD*). The BFS *knows* with her irrational body that mastery is a futile pursuit. For the BFS, 'Sat in Your Lap' is a moment of ontological breakdown. That is, a fundamental breakdown at the level of being. This breakdown is also a breakthrough (albeit a nervous one). The rest of the album follows on from this revelation.

Becoming 1. Becoming Machine

> *Leave it Open* is the idea of human beings being like cups - like receptive vessels. We open and shut ourselves at different times. It's very easy to let your ego go 'nag nag nag' when you should shut it. Or when you're very narrow-minded and you should be open. Finally you should be able to control your levels of receptivity to a productive end.[5]

In the above quotation Bush reflects on the ways humans control how much they are open or closed. It asks how can we be receptive to our environment if we are not open to interaction with the world around us. This is a fundamental shift towards becoming explored by the BFS on *The Dreaming*. Becoming is an empathetic, expansive act and pivots on issues of receptivity and interconnectivity. At a basic level, it is about being open to the world.

The BFS in 'Leave it Open' is in process. She is inside the micro-processes of perception as she opens and closes her eyes, exploring the basic instinct of being alive. The song becomes a head, a body and then a number of bodies dramatised through the BFS's voices, fleshes, technologies and interconnections. The BFS is always multiple.

The song sees the BFS struggle with her bodily and psychic thresholds. She is permeated by the knowledge and fear of pain. Infiltrated by images of violence and harm, 'Leave it Open' dramatises the consequences of confronting violence within oneself. This is presented as an ethical struggle. It is one that must be broken through in order to move into new spaces of awareness.

The song begins by the BFS closing herself off from the world. She asserts her boundaries in order to ward off invasion from outside forces: 'With my ego in my gut/ My babbling mouth would wash it up/ (But now I've started *learning* how)/ I keep it shut' (*TD*, italics mine). The BFS has been afflicted by an injury evoked by the 'trigger come – cocking' (*TD*). This has made her unreceptive or hostile to outside forces, 'My door was never locked' (*TD*): when previously she had been 'open.' When these lines are sung, the initial vocal line is heavily affected to give it a metallic, dehumanising quality. In these lyrics I have chosen to italicise the word 'learning.' This suggests a continuous and processual development that occurs throughout the song. On record these lines are delivered in repetitious squeaky echoes which distinguish them from the other voices and instruments.

The closing-off in the song occurs at the physical level of the body. This is expressed as a type of perception. The eyes form a point of access through which to experience compassion and insight but this threshold is subject to disintegration: 'things that decay, things that rust' (*TD*).

'Leave it Open' is a combination of organic and inorganic dissolution, both of which are the consequence of neglect.

The chorus marks the beginning of the shift towards a different positioning of the boundaries between self and other. This is awakened by an ethical confrontation with pain which propels the BFS. As more voices enter into the song's body, the chorus is chanted like a mantra by layers of male vocals: 'Harm is in *us*,/ Harm in *us* but power to arm' (*TD*, italics mine). This begins to open up previously closed structures.

The collision with 'harm' attempts to activate collective memory. It displays a willingness to assume cultural responsibility for inflicting violence upon others. 'Leave it Open' is about shocking de-sensitised senses back into action. It is about being aware at the level of *feeling* (as opposed to intellectual knowledge) of the possibilities of personal and cultural violence: 'I kept it in a cage,/ Watched it weeping, but I made it stay/ (but now I've started learning how)/ I leave it open' (*TD*).

These lyrics describe the detached violence of the BFS watching another person or animal in pain and incarceration. They are a confession while claiming responsibility – 'I made it stay.' In the 'I leave it open' statement there is movement away from static guilt to a more open framework.

The finale to 'Leave it Open' is an epic explosion and implosion of the contained space that begins the song. The 'Harm is in us' mantra gathers pace, drowning in a sonic theatre of previously unacknowledged collective violence: the harm 'in us.' The song stages a confrontation. Repetitions build layers which communicate the possibility of integrating an awareness of violence. Heavy drums drive through barriers, layers of screaming collapse and fold on top of one another. Thresholds are broken, crossed and traversed: 'Harm is in us/ Harm in you and me' (*TD*). While she asks 'What are you letting in?/ Tell me what you're letting in/ Say what we're gonna let in/ We let the weirdness in' (*TD*).

The relative stability of boundaries, maintained by avoiding receptivity and containing others, is broken apart in this final section. This will have consequences for the BFS. The ending of the song enacts the process of merging and becoming. It makes known the point where one entity interacts or collides with another which creates new subjectivities; 'Fibres lead us from one to the other, transform one into the other as they pass through doors and across thresholds.'[6] These forces connect to other forms. They splinter and create sounds and positions in between the connections. This is the consequence when 'weirdness' or difference is let in, transforming the contours of the BFS.

'Leave it Open' is a statement that champions the liberation from structural confinement. Nevertheless, this refusal to enslave or cage up is not a pain-free process. The song demonstrates this. Opening things up erodes stability and control and wears away the ground of exclusion that keeps 'our selves,' as individuals, safe from harm of 'the other.' The reality of *The Dreaming* as a whole states that this is neither possible nor desirable. Entities cannot be kept separate, no matter how hard the BFS tries.

The Dreaming radically pushes the boundaries of sonic perception. It creates new knowledge and ways of relating to enfleshed sound. The production of the album carries an 'insist[ence] on noise' that 'advocate[s] pollution, rejoicing in the illegitimate fusions of animal and machine.'[7] This ensures that new connections are rendered physical, sonic, material. The reworking of relationships produces radically new perceptions which pass through thresholds and leave questions open.

Becoming 2. 'The Dreaming'

'The Dreaming' is another space of becoming for the BFS as she tries to become post-colonial. The song attempts to comment on, and condemn, the historical and contemporary violence of white colonial settlers in Australia. It does not seek to represent the voice of Aboriginal people in Australia. The song remains *about* their struggles. Yet, it does not perpetuate colonial stereotypes that exoticise or festishise difference like she does in 'Kashka from Baghdad.'

In the song the BFS stays close to her own limited perspective. She tells her story of British colonialism in Australia in her voices. This of course is itself not free from contestation. As a woman, the BFS will struggle her whole life to speak on her own terms within a male-dominated world. We have seen part of her battle already in the journey, and it will continue throughout the book. However, she does have privilege as a white woman and this grants her power as well.

If the BFS can be said to reside in a single location on 'The Dreaming' (which would be very difficult to do), then it would be as a witness to British colonial history. In this way she is similar to Donna Haraway's 'modest witness.' Haraway describes that 'my Modest Witness cannot ever be simply oppositional. Rather s/he is suspicious, implicated, knowing, ignorant, worried, and hopeful.'[8]

The modest witnessing of the BFS means she is implicated in colonial history as much as she seeks to challenge it. Due to her position as a white British woman she can never claim to be wholly opposed or removed. She can't be. Culturally she inherits this involvement. She remains entwined within 'the net of stories, agencies and instruments'[9] that constitute her colonially-mediated historical reality. The BFS is implicated in the colonial narrative of the song. At the same time, the critique she presents (and the way she presents it) distances her from colonial abuses.

The BFS does open up a crucial space where a Western based critique of the colonial situation in Australia can emerge. As she commented at the time:

> for many years it has greatly disturbed me, the way 'civilised' man has treated ancient tribes such as the Aborigines, Red Indians, Tasmanians... and because of the beauty of the Aborigines' music and the way it seems to exude space, and the feeling of having great contact with the earth, I felt it was the perfect way to portray this feeling of invasion by white man.[10]

The Dreaming as a whole mixes up sounds from all around the world, including many indigenous instruments. In 'The Dreaming' the use of the didgeridoo is a prominent feature. It is played by the white Australian musician and artist Rolf Harris. His 1960s song 'Sunrise' first introduced Bush to the instrument. We should not forget that the use of this instrument still lies in a shadow of white cultural appropriation.

The indigenous people of Australia do have a presence in the song but this is not in a lyrical form. Instead this presence is communicated through the non-representational use of sound. The BFS uses sound art and the didgeridoo to do this. The didgeridoo is described earlier as exuding space, carrying the ability to create a feeling of connectivity with the land. Highlighting the land is important because in Aboriginal Dreamtime philosophy; 'land is the mediating agency between the world of the ancestors and the world of living human beings. Land, spirit and the living are inseparable.'[11]

'The Dreaming' imagines an experience of the Australian outback. It creates an atmospheric, physical and sensory soundscape. There are no specific dates mentioned but it does seem to be based in the contemporary setting of the 1980s. It also evokes previous historical events. The present is suggested because the architecture of colonial settlement is well in place. 'The motorway' (*TD*), the presence of western technologies and 'the bonnet of the van' (*TD*) are essential parts of this soundscape. These are heightened by the use of screeching car noises made courtesy of the Fairlight Synthesizer.

The song presents the landscape's more alienating aspects. It is narrated from the perspective of the British person as s/he is estranged there. The song is saturated with fear and displacement. Australia is presented as a landscape of volatile and unpredictable forces: "Bang' goes another Kanga/ On the bonnet of the van' (*TD*). While 'Many an aborigine's mistaken for a tree/ 'Til you near him on the motorway,/ The tree begin to breathe' (*TD*).

Guns bang. Roaming kangaroos dent the bonnets of vans. There is confusion as seemingly inanimate forces start to breathe and move. Anxiety is expressed as the hissing of breath signals trees coming to life. The brown of tree bark and the brown of human skin merge, creating camouflage for the Aboriginal people.

Breath is an important rhythm in the song. It forms part of the percussion and makes us aware of the embodied nature of music-making. The promotional video to the song conveys this. The BFS is seen stomping around 'Australia' in a bizarre kind of space suit engaged in this visceral breathing, delivering her lines in a fake-Aussie accent. Breath is an important tactic of the BFS. It is part of making known the 'culture of breath' that Irigaray describes as essential for creating a culture of sexual difference.[12] Rhythmically, the song mimics the digging up of the land. This is consistent throughout: 'Dig, dig, dig away' (*TD*).

The song is told from the perspective of the British colonisers. However, it is told in such away to encourage listeners to see the irony and futility of the colonial 'mission': 'Coming in with the golden light is the New Man./ Coming in with the golden light is my dented van' (*TD*). The 'golden light' of progress is undermined through the inclusion of the 'dented van.' This strategy is continued in the second verse. We remain resident in the colonial psyche: 'The civilised keep alive the territorial war/ (See the light ram through the gaps in the land)' (*TD*). Their objectives are spoken: 'Erase the race that claim the place/ And say we dig for ore/ Or dangle Devils in a bottle/ And push them from the Pull of the Bush' (*TD*).

Here there is no attempt to cast judgment upon those who are keeping alive the 'territorial war.' Instead it is the listener's responsibility to discern the unjust nature of this statement. The song becomes immersed in the ruthless pursuit of resources at all costs. It follows the call to 'erase the race.' This lays bare the colonial logic which exterminates whatever gets in the way of the pursuit 'for ore.'

Juxtaposed with the main colonial narrative is an alternative voice that emerges in the song. This moves toward a celebration of land and light. This voice 'ram[s] through the gaps in the land,' and 'bounce[s] off the rocks to the sand' (*TD*). These lines are written and contained within brackets on the lyric sheet. On the record they are sung in a high arching tone. They are inserted behind the primary vocal which delivers the narrative.

The entrance of this voice signals a shift in the song. It is the beginning of a process where the combination of voices, words, breath and noises create a sense of light and nature. They attempt to communicate the spirituality of the land and Aboriginal mythology. These sonic textures eventually overwhelm the colonial voice in the song. This further heightens the sense of alienation, displacement and eventually engulfment.

The song is a circle. It subsumes narratives of progression and linearity. Phrases are repeated. They drown out any attempt to present the colonial domination of Australia as a justifiable enterprise. The repetition acts as a kind of mental panic on behalf of the colonial voice. Its attempts at cohesion radically fall apart. The result is the disintegration of the song into observant and desperate phrases: 'You find them in the road/ In the road/ (See the light)/ Pull of the Bush' (*TD*).

It is the 'Pull of the Bush' that endures in the song rather than attempts to pillage its resources. Listeners are encouraged to 'See the Light' (*TD*). This is communicated when the primary vocal is displaced, smothered by layers of sonic light. 'The Dreaming' moves into an understanding where relationships with the world are not ruled by opposition to people and space.

Dreamtime is the central unifying theme in Aboriginal mythology. It is said to be the oldest continuously maintained cultural history on earth. It also diverges from Western liberal humanist ideology which *The Dreaming* is similarly at odds with. This divergence is situated in its treatment of history, time and relationship to surroundings:

> Living Aborigines are tied to land and spirit in the most complex way which includes their kinship with Ancestors, the land for which they act as caretakers and guardians, and their inextricable connection with all that exists on that land. Everything is interconnected in a vast web of sacredness.[13]

In 'The Dreaming' this sense of Aboriginal culture gains its position as the final 'voice' or presence in the song. This is communicated through the technique of layering noises. The final section of the song sees the

BFS revelling within a pioneering moment of sound art. As voices subside there is an initial sonic blanket of car noises. These are cleared away by a thrash of drums. Through the collision of noise emerges the drone of the didgeridoo which has remained constant throughout the song. Now it is highlighted by being placed at the front of the mix.

The rhythmical digging remains a regular feature of the song. The drone of the didgeridoo is complemented by animal noises. The beating of bird wings as they fly away merges with the pleasant sound of birdsong. This communicates the imagined natural sound of the landscape. It is symbolic of the sense of freedom and flight that is so important to the song that follows, 'Night of the Swallow.' The final words of the song are spoken in an Aboriginal language. Allegedly 'it's a lyric from a song called Airplane! Airplane! And it's very strange because it's one of the first Aboriginal songs about airplanes.'[14]

Through the process of the song the BFS attempts to create a space where an Aboriginal voice is articulated. At the same time 'The Dreaming' displays an understanding of the difficulty of colonised people having a political voice and offers a variety of sonic strategies to comment on this. Through the use of sound art the song underscores the limits of lyrical representation, counteracting it with sonic textures to create a politicised sense of space and sound.

The endurance of the droning didgeridoo is important in the song, and the album as a whole. It breaks out of the space and containment that a song usually delimits. As the Aboriginal voice finishes its lyrics, the drone continues. It acts as an interconnection and extension of the space of the song. That is until it also fades with the entrance of the Irish refrain of 'Night of the Swallow.'

Becoming 3. 'Night of the Swallow'. Becoming Irish/ Swallow

'Night of the Swallow' contains a double becoming, becoming Irish and becoming swallow. It is important to remember that 'one becomes [...] no less than the one that becomes.'[15] In other words becomings are always expansive, they never take away subjectivity. They produce more than what existed before the encounter.

The 'becoming Irish' of 'Night of the Swallow' is part of a general attempt on the album to become post-colonial. This tries to move away from the exclusive and exclusionary identity that the BFS began her life with. You will most clearly remember this from *Lionheart*. The BFS is often thought of as synonymous with musical allusions to Irish and Celtic folk traditions; but it was not until *The Dreaming* that these sounds came to occupy a central place in the body of her work.

The instance of becoming Irish in 'Night of the Swallow' emerges through the inclusion of Irish folk sounds in the song. Bush commented: 'I've wanted to work with Irish music for years, but my writing has never really given me the opportunity of doing so until now.'[16] On 'Night of the Swallow' the drone of the didgeridoo from 'The Dreaming' merges into the sound of Uillean Pipes, penny whistle, fiddle and Bouzouki. The latter is an instrument that despite its Greek origins has become a mainstay of Irish traditional music since the 60s.

A traditional Irish arrangement introduces the song, with sounds that are evocative of a boat being removed from its mooring. The music sails gently into the unfolding soundscape. The Irish refrain is used to conjure the sense of flying, simulating the winding-up of an aeroplane propeller. This is one manifestation of the multiple flights that occur within the song. On 'Night of the Swallow' Irish music signifies the uncategorisable space of the middle, the neither-here-nor-there feeling of flying between places.

The narrative drama of the song is based on conflict between a female and a male lover. The woman tries to stop her partner from flying refugees by night because she deems it too dangerous for him. The act of flying, or the journey, is similar to the process of becoming. It is 'the in-between, the border line or line of flight'[17] mentioned in the song: 'They hold the sky/ On the other side/ Of border lines' (*TD*).

As I described at the beginning of the chapter, there is no narrator explaining the story or introducing the characters. This is a shift in the story-telling strategy that characterises much of *The Dreaming*. We are simply immersed in the drama of their situation. The song switches between the perspectives of the male and female characters. We gain an appreciation of who is speaking through alternative uses of voice, communicated through pitch and timbre. This also occurs within the spatial positioning of the vocals in the final mix.

Initially the male character in the song is granted the ability to fly. The Irish music provides him with elevation and flight within the music. This refrain grants the speaker safety and protection. He assures his lover that: 'With a hired plane/ And no names mentioned [...] Before you know/ I'll be over the water like a swallow' (*TD*).

The female character is however largely kept on the ground. When she is enveloped in the flight, it is seemingly against her will. There is not the rhythmical, galloping euphoria that is connected to the male character. He is able to revel in the danger and excitement of his illegal adventures. There is ambiguity surrounding the question of whether the female character is granted flight at all. As the two perspectives merge in the climactic point of the song it is unclear who is speaking: 'Would you break even my wings/ Just like a swallow/ Let me, let me go/ But you're not a swallow' (*TD*).

The female character voices her reservations. She attempts to place restrictions on movement and invokes authority: 'If you go, I'll let the law know/ And they'll head you off when you touch the ground' (*TD*). Although the song challenges ideas about space and borders, the traditional borders between genders remain in place. That is if the genders of the speakers in the song are to be taken literally, because in *The Dreaming*, *everything* is destabilised. 'Night of the Swallow,' with its preoccupation with borderlines and displacement, does provide alternative strategies to experience space and motion within a song. This disorders both the BFS and the listener's movement within space and time.

The inclusion of an Irish refrain on 'Night of the Swallow' contributes to the overall hybridity of *The Dreaming*. This hybridity is important because it disrupts cultural ideas of purity which are underpinned by the desire to keep identities separate, uncontaminated and stable. If we remember how the BFS had previously claimed that 'everything she does is English,' this demonstrates an important shift in how she relates to her own identity. Through this hybridity the inter-mixture of the BFS is announced.

As a strategy, hybridity can be used to critique the organization of knowledge systems in the West. Philosopher Rosi Braidotti argues these systems are 'based on the ontology of Sameness or the Rule of One. This includes a dualistic relationship to the rest of the human race [...] The power of sameness in the west is best described in terms of monolinguism, or the illusion of a single cultural and linguistic root.'[18]

The Dreaming contains a wide variety of sounds, voices and positions. It radically challenges the idea of a single root forming the basis of the work. It is an inter-mixture of forms in action. This is not to say that there is no unity to the work. The unity emerges from its disjunctions, multiplicities and multi-vocality. The music is determined to not remain within closed structures. They are opened up. Disjunctions are placed next to each other in order to produce new configurations.

It is not only the music of place and region that contributes to 'Night of the Swallow's hybridity. This also occurs with the becoming of the swallow that the music enacts. The music becomes like the body of a bird, beating its wings, flying and swooping. According to many folk traditions, the swallow 'is a natural symbol of hope, new life and good fortune, while the hope symbolism is stressed in that, descending from the sky, it took the form of an anchor.'[19] Swallows are tattooed onto prisoners' necks and hands to symbolise freedom. They are also a traditional nautical symbol of good luck for travellers trying to find their way home. The use of the symbol is linked with the desire for the safety of the male character's homecoming in the song.

The becoming of the swallow is created in the chorus as the flight begins to take off. The drums echo the rhythm of flapping wings. The BFS's vocals, most strikingly communicated by the low 'oooohs,' create an impression of the swallow swooping and diving through the sky. This is exaggerated by more vocals that intensify the sense of plunging. The movement pans from left to right speakers, creating a further instance of motion. The BFS's whole body is in flight. The BFS is becoming swallow.

What is remarkable about the song is how it inhabits the space of the swallow and communicates its movement. The song does not *imitate* the swallow. Becoming is never 'a resemblance, an imitation, or, at the limit, an identification.'[20] To do this would replicate a man-made image of the swallow. It would never be able to break into the space it inhabits or weave in and out of its patterns of flight. Becoming swallow in the song is about forming a close enough relation. This is becoming as 'a block of co-existence.'[21] It is a space of transformation for both parties. Becoming is a strategy that nurtures interconnection with other, surrounding, human and non-human life. The 'space of becoming is a space of affinity and correlation of elements, among compatible and mutually attractive forces.'[22]

The significance of the swallow is as a vehicle of flight within the song. It is simultaneously mechanic and natural. Its path merges with the plane the pilot is flying. Through the swallow's body the listener experiences flight. This flight is strained and ambivalent. The restrictions placed on the bird, pilot and refugees is an important dramatic device in the song. 'In Malta, catch a swallow/ For all of the guilty to set them free/ Wings fill the window/ As they beat and bleed' (*TD*).

The imagery of ensnaring the birds and the desire to liberate 'the guilty' creates tension. The *capacity* for free, intuitive movement unquestionably grates against the *restrictions* placed on this movement. This occurs on two levels in the song. Firstly in the woman and man's relationship and her desire to not let him move where he wants. Secondly, by including refugees in the song, a category produced by the invention of borders that some are allowed to cross while others are not.

In 'Night of the Swallow' the ability to cross borders freely becomes an extreme privilege when it should be a fundamental freedom that everybody has. The violence that arises from placing restrictions on movement becomes apparent. The swallows become a swarm of birds, fighting back with their broken and bleeding bodies: 'Give me something to take/ Would you break even my wings,/ Just like a Swallow/ Let me, let me go' (*TD*).

Musically, this tension makes the movement within the music's movement only more intense. There is a sense of elevation and of flight rarely created within a song. It fluxes through its darting terrain. The communication of such a physical sense of movement enables the listener to also move into new spaces and across thresholds. These can only be accessed by allowing living creatures the freedom to move where they *need* to go.

Breakdown 2.
'Get out of My House' and the body in pain

The last song on *The Dreaming*, 'Get out of My House', presents a very angry woman removing a male presence from her home. He has violently invaded her spatial and psychic boundaries. 'Get out of My House,' like so much of *The Dreaming*, is a song about thresholds. The last song on album, it pushes them to the limit of sonic and expressive capability.

In the song the house is a metaphor for the woman's body. A brutally loud reclamation of her internal and external boundaries is waged. The sonic textures in the song collide with one another. The body of the BFS becomes a battleground.

The metaphorical correspondence between the female body and the house is one that women writers have invoked before. Cixous commented in the 1970s, woman has

> not been able to live in her 'own' house, her very body. She can be incarcerated, slowed down appallingly and tricked into apartheid for too long a time--but still only for a time. . . . We have internalized this fear of the dark. Women haven't had eyes for themselves. They haven't gone exploring in their house.[23]

Cixous uses the metaphor of the house to evoke female experience, expression and sexuality. These have not been explored or given viable space to flourish within male-dominated culture. Crucially, the house has also functioned historically as a kind of prison for women, confining them to the domestic realm. Woman occupies a phantom residence in her own body/house.

Cixous' use of quotation marks around 'own' suggests we should be aware that the house is essentially a male-defined concept. It is connected to other systems of property ownership, existing within a system of capital and exchange. In this exchange women have been one of the most important commodities.

In her influential essay, 'The Traffic in Women,' Gayle Rubin describes how women are connected to these systems. She outlines the 'systematic social apparatus which takes up females as raw materials and fashions domesticated women as products.'[24] She argues this system of exchange is what all women's bodies are subject to. Therefore, being confined to the male-defined space of the house prevents women from exploring their own bodies, rhythms, desires and destinies.

The BFS's treatment of the house attends to these problems. It dramatises a woman gaining control over her domestic space but as she does this she also crucially *reorders* the boundaries of that space. The song emphasises that asserting the right to self-determination and definition is no easy task for women. This is due to the prolonged male occupation of female space within culture. The song is faithful to this. It promises any struggle will not be made without vocalising pain, distress and disorientation. Without these factors, genuine transformation cannot occur.

The BFS in 'Get out of My House' is also traumatised. She cannot articulate her pain in a solely coherent manner. Instead she vocalises her anguish through a combination of tactics. She grunts. She screams. She shouts. She is poetic. She makes animal noises. Despite the fact the BFS communicates her bodily violation very clearly; she still remains distanced from the subject. This is because her distress is expressed through the medium of metaphor. The BFS's body is not her own body. Her body is a house. She sings 'No stranger's feet/ Will enter me/ I wash the panes/ I clean the stains' (*TD*).

Her need to clean her house is similar to the need to cleanse the body after experiencing sexual violation. The image of cleaning the window panes and physical dirt in the house provides an external focus for pain experienced internally and pushes that pain away. The use of the house as a metaphor provides a vehicle for articulating pain that perhaps could not be expressed in any other way. This is a technique that resonates with theories of trauma that suggest it is difficult to express the gravity of such an experience directly in language.

The metaphor of the house, with its relatively stable structural capacity to lock people out of it, provides a strong symbol from which to assert the boundary that will not be violated any longer: 'I am the concierge, chez moi, honey/ Won't letcha in for love nor money,' for it is 'My home, my joy,/ I'm barred and bolted and I/ Won't letcha in' (*TD*).

In the song these lines are sung by one of many different voices. They make up the multiple selves that are housed within the body of the BFS. These voices also become part of the internal architecture of the house as doors slam and lock. It is as if the BFS has many personalities. This furthers the sense of disorientation for the listener. It pushes them to contend with the terrifying, but cathartic, experience dramatised in the song. It enables us to also *become traumatised* as we are attacked by the various voices that are part of the BFS's reality: 'With my keeper I (clean it up)/ With my keeper I (clean it all up) (*TD*).

The use of the term 'keeper' is suggestive of the presence of a kind of carer. It can also represent another dimension of the BFS's consciousness. She is desperately trying to restore some sense of balance. The house is saturated with pervasive disorder: 'This house is full of m-m my mess/ This house is full of m-m my mistakes/ This house is full of m-m my madness/ This house is full of, full of, full of, full of fight' (*TD*).

Stammering re-creates the difficulty traumatised people have in expressing themselves coherently. However the last line sees the BFS virulently articulate her defiance. She does this in the face of all her imperfections; her mess, mistakes and madness which have all been deemed typically female and feminine qualities. They have been used to justify the exclusion of women from the position where they can be viable contributors to cultural production.[25]

'Get out of My House' showcases the power of women's irrationality. This is an important quality of the BFS. You will remember how she has previously championed such behaviour. Voicing these 'disorders' lends the BFS's 'madness' a powerful sense of cultural legitimacy. She does this not only for herself, but for other women as well.

Ann Cvetkovich defines trauma 'as a social and cultural discourse that emerges in response to the demands of grappling with the psychic consequences of historical events.'[26] Trauma emerges then, as response to the type of experiences people have to the culture they live in. It is not an *individual* illness, but arises in response to events and experience. Depending on your cultural background, it will increase or decrease your chances of being traumatised by living in pervasively sexist, racist, classist and homophobic culture.

Within a male dominated culture, women are the most likely to experience trauma. This can be seen not only in 'Get out of My House,' but *The Dreaming* as a whole. These can be large scale traumas such as sexual violence, or the more everyday trauma that builds up over time. These traumas, for example, can arise from a lack of cultural spaces or opportunities. Often women have had prescribed roles imposed on them (such as wife and mother). These have encouraged them to sacrifice and negate both their power and their personal will and desire. These imposed destinies are a kind of violence. They prevent people from living lives of 'persistence and flourishing'[27] which should be a baseline necessity for all.

In 'Get out of My House' the BFS *is* able to articulate her anguish in a complex and sophisticated manner through the use of metaphor. This is facilitated by the innovative use of studio technologies which communicate her distressed, multiple perspectives. The BFS is able to articulate powerful sites of trauma that exist within the bodily landscape of a woman who has been violated. She marks this trauma on her own body.

This pain does not remain *within* her body. It is pushed outwards. The house in the song is not the singular home of one traumatised but fighting female subject. It also represents the eruption of long silenced and previously contained, collective female anger. The song is the sound of these women fighting back: 'This house is old as I am/ This house knows all I have done' (*TD*).

The finale to the song is the point where male voices attempt to re-enter the BFS's previously secured boundaries. A vocal duel takes place between the male and female voices. The male voice can be seen to evoke a traumatic memory that continues to haunt the speaker amidst her mess: 'Woman let me in/ Let me bring in the memories/ Woman let me in/ Let me bring in the Devil Dreams' (*TD*).

This last sequence suggests that the traumatic memory will never fully be removed from the BFS's reality. It has become lodged in her body, forming a crucial part of her experience. As the BFS is under siege, she remains defiant. She pushes away the presence of the unwanted house guest: 'I will not let you in/ I face toward the wind,/ I change into the Mule./ 'Hee – Haw' (*TD*).

Here resistance to the male speaker escapes reasonable bargaining. He is not able to understand the requests of the BFS to get out of her house and stay out. In response, the BFS devises other strategies of resistance. These do not rely on the supposedly logical and egalitarian tools of language. The BFS undergoes a metamorphic transformation into a mule which symbolises her stubborn refusal to give in her fight. In the process she utilises the realm of the imagination as a means of resistance. It creates a space where she can escape traumatic pursuit.

'Get Out of My House' produces a seething and dynamic space in which to explore the traumatised mind and body of the BFS. She gives powerful testimony to this experience. She occupies the house for the duration of the song and dramatically re-orders its spatial, sensory and psychic boundaries. This allows the BFS to reclaim the house as her own, her body as her own. As listeners we become embroiled in the interior mechanics of the house. We see how it re-articulates traumatic experience.

The result is to highlight both the house and the woman's body as an actual cultural site on which trauma occurs. It is not just that women are mad. Male-defined culture is also. 'Get Out of My House' refuses to use the boundaries of the house as a silencing mechanism. Instead it uses this metaphor to explore the depth and dimensions of traumatic experience. It is an example of a productive expression of the body in pain as it is sung through the body of the BFS.

The Dreaming: dancing in the ruins

The Dreaming has seen the BFS undergo powerful changes. They have been achieved through a series of breakdowns and becomings which significantly re-ordered her life. The process has seen her redefine her music and herself along the way. The way she embraced technological innovations made her nosier, angrier and more uncompromising than ever before. On *The Dreaming* the BFS engaged with messy and difficult subjects. She created a space where she could confront her own and others' violence, seeking transformation as she did so.

The album is the BFS's attempt to also move into radically different political terrains from the ones that coloured her early life. 'Leave it Open,' 'Night of the Swallow' and 'The Dreaming' all explore these issues in different ways. On 'The Dreaming' she engages with critique of Britain's colonial ventures. Even if she cannot stand outside this history she finds ways of challenging it, particularly through pioneering uses of sound art. Both 'Sat in Your Lap' and 'Get Out of My House' articulate resistance to the enclosure of male power upon knowledge and women's bodies respectively. They re-order rhythm, space and time as they do so.

The good news for readers is that the pain-saturated, disorientating challenge of *The Dreaming* is over now. The BFS will undergo new challenges and changes in the next chapter that will have their own unique difficulties. In the next chapter we will leap ahead in time nearly 10 years to *The Red Shoes* and *The Line, the Cross and the Curve*. It is here that we will negotiate the death of the BFS.

The Red Shoes and the death of the BFS

From the creative ruins of 1982's *The Dreaming*, we now leap forward eleven years in the BFS's life to consider her place within the story of 'The Red Shoes.' *The Red Shoes* and *The Line, the Cross and the Curve* mark an important coming of age for the BFS. More accurately, it marks a coming of death, symbolised by her choice to wear the red shoes.

For women, wearing red shoes is not a decision to be taken lightly. It results in certain death - death through dancing, possession by art. The BFS's fate is no different. Her negotiation of the story is an important struggle within its narrow possibility. This chapter is dedicated to exploring *how* the BFS, who is, we should remember, a great storyteller, challenges the story of 'The Red Shoes.'

To do this we will begin by looking at the versions of the tale that were written before she offered her intervention. We will be considering in particular how the BFS creates space for the main female character to tell the story in her own voice and on her own terms. These are familiar strategies of the BFS from early in her life. Much of *The Kick Inside*, you will recall, is about claiming a space for the independent female voice to stand up and be counted.

You will also need to remember another important thing about the BFS that we covered in chapter one: that she has the special power to be reborn. With the BFS, after death there will always be birth. So even if she does effectively kill herself by choosing to wear the red shoes, this death is only ever temporary. She will emerge again within the cycles of birth and death as is her (birth) right and inclination.

Hans Christian Andersen's 'The Red Shoes'

Both the album *The Red Shoes*, and the film, *The Line, The Cross and the Curve* (1993) rewrite Hans Christian Andersen's tale, 'The Red Shoes.' The original story was published in England in 1845 at the height of the fairy tale revival. Fairy tales became popular in mid-nineteenth century as a tool of social control. These stories taught people the cultural values of society that must be adhered to, at a time when vast social and economic changes were afoot because of the industrial revolution. It was what Angela Carter called 'the most fundamental change in human culture since the Iron Age – the final divorce from the land.'[1]

Fairy tales of the nineteenth century reflected bourgeois value systems as they were emerging. They promoted the moral standards which served the interests of property owning, Christian, male-dominated classes. These fairy tales were particularly cruel towards young girls, as my relaying of 'The Red Shoes' story itself in a moment, will demonstrate.

Fairy tales were not nice or innocent. For the most part they were ideological and violent towards girl's bodies that they sought to control. There were exceptions, as both the Brontë sisters and Christina Rossetti used fairy tales in a subversive way, for example.[2] On the most part fairy tales are what Maria Tatar describes as 'cautionary tales' which 'persuade children to obey laws set down by parental authority, celebrating docility and conformity while discouraging curiosity and wilfulness.'[3]

This is particularly true for the original tale of 'The Red Shoes.' The tale is a grave warning for any girls who are seduced by their own vanity and desire for material possessions. For the main character Karen, the much coveted red shoes are her weak point and they remain the enduring image of the story. The shoes continue to dance with Karen's feet still in them after they have been cut from her body, haunting her and the story to the end: '...she confessed all her sin, and the executioner struck off her feet with the red shoes; but the shoes danced away with the little feet over the fields and into the deep forest.'[4] Ultimately the message of 'The Red Shoes' is to keep girls in their place; a place where they are obedient and still.

The first day Karen wears red shoes is at her mother's funeral. This is a fact of great symbolic importance. Bruno Bettleheim suggests, 'many fairy stories begin with the death of a mother or father.'[5] The narrator informs us that these shoes 'were certainly not suited for mourning; but she had no others.'[6] Wearing the shoes at such an inappropriate time, signals Karen's first violation of the social codes that encase and eventually undo her. To not mourn in a suitably morose fashion is to offend the Christian morality integral to the tale's lesson.

As the story develops, Karen is depicted as obsessively driven by her desire for the red shoes. They overpower her, leading her to dispense with all logic and care; 'Nothing in the world can compare with red shoes!'[7] After her first pair of red shoes is destroyed, Karen is able to acquire another pair for her confirmation ceremony. It is after this event that the power of the shoes escalates and it is clear that Karen's disobedience has gone too far. Karen encounters a soldier who casts a spell over the shoes that compels them to dance: '"Look, what beautiful dancing shoes!" and Karen could not resist; she was obliged to dance a few steps; and when she once began, her legs went on dancing.'[8] Eventually the shoes force her out into the woods where she encounters the soldier again. This is the beginning of her dance for brutal liberation. She attempts to pull the shoes off,

> but they stuck fast. And she tore off her stockings; but the shoes had grown fast to her feet. And she danced and was compelled to go dancing over field and meadow, in rain and sunshine, by night and by day; but by night it was most horrible.[9]

Eventually she dances into a churchyard, and it is here that she sees an angel wielding a sword who decrees her fate:

> [To] dance in your red shoes till thou are pale and cold, till thy body shrivels and you are a skeleton! Dance you shall, from door to door, and where proud, haughty chil-

> dren dwell you shall knock, that they may hear thee and be afraid of thee. Dance you shall, dance!'"[10]

Dancing is transformed from a pleasurable and liberating activity to a state of personal and communal terror. The message not only warns of the dangers of vanity, but instils fear into the act of dancing itself. This punishment for movement also places a taboo on physical expression in general, and in particular the excess of female sexuality, as Karen becomes a scapegoat for the vulgarity of these acts.

Eventually the relentless dancing proves too much for Karen. She is danced to the house of the executioner. She begs him to not cut off her head '"for then I could not repent of my sin."'[11] Instead he cuts off her feet. Karen is given a pair of wooden shoes and crutches by the executioner and she returns to the town and repents. One Sunday morning Karen is subject to heavenly intervention that ends her misery once and for all:

> Then the sun shone so brightly; and right before her stood an angel of God in white garments; the same one she had seen that night at the church-door. But he no longer carried the sharp sword, but a beautiful green branch, full of roses; and he touched the ceiling, which rose up very high, and wherever he had touched it a golden star streamed forth. He touched the walls, and they spread forth widely, and she saw the organ which was pealing its rich sounds.[12]

Karen, forbidden to go to church because of her sins, is now granted access to the congregation through the divine powers of the angel. She can now die a happy and merciful death. As her soul flies up to heaven the revelatory moment occurs, 'her heart became so filled with sunshine, peace and joy, that it broke.'[13] The cruel celebration of her sin and repentance that the tale dramatises is complete. Karen is only allowed to die because she has suffered and displayed an awareness of the need for suffering.

I have spent some time outlining the original story of 'The Red

Shoes' because it is important for understanding how the BFS will make her challenge to the story. It contains the key images, actions and symbols that are alluded to when she tells her version of it. 'The Red Shoes' as a symbol and story did not end with Andersen's tale. When he wrote the tale he created a powerful symbolic universe that other artists, writers and film-makers would pick up and use again and again. Each subsequent version of the tale would rework and expand upon its symbolism and meaning, securing the centrality of the tale within the popular cultural imaginary.

Part of the attraction of the tale is Andersen's success at instilling a spirit of danger and taboo within the symbol of the shoes. He does this by juxtaposing the sanctity of bodily and spiritual sobriety, against the intoxication and indulgence of the red shoes. This means the shoes will always be seductive to readers who have sympathy with excess and transgression. In the past 150 years red shoes and dancing have become symbols of all the things which are rejected by the religiously fundamentalist, male dominated imaginary. It is these exuberant qualities that characterise Powell and Pressburger's 1948 cinematic interpretation of the tale.

The 1948 film version of The Red Shoes

One hundred years after the original tale became part of culture, the Archer's[14] voluptuous art-house picture *The Red Shoes* was released in 1948. The film, shot in shimmering deep colour, helped cleanse the debris from the British post-war imagination. They moved Karen's story out of the church and into the dance rehearsal room, exchanging dour Christian morality for high camp antics. In fact, the worlds in which the two versions are set could not be more different, as the opulent spirit of the red shoes is breathed everywhere into the decadent but cut-throat world of modern ballet. Nonetheless, the principal female character still receives her punishment as a result of wearing the red shoes. This suggests that wearing the shoes remains an act entangled in the grip of punishment and eternal damnation inherent to the story.

Explicitly based on Andersen's tale, the opening and closing shots of the film show the book lit by the candle. 'The Red Shoes' in fact operates as a 'tale within a tale,' as the film dramatises the adaptation of the story with all the action building towards the opening night of a balletic version of 'The Red Shoes.' Its depictions of the rehearsals, the writing of the music, and the heated directorial meetings, embroil viewers in the dramatic process of putting on a world-class ballet show.

The Archer's film includes a cinematic rendition of Karen's story. Memorable scenes include the frantic dream sequences that communicate her inner world which, in turn, merge with the story of Victoria Page, the main female character in the film. The balletic interpretation of 'The Red Shoes' provides much of the visual imagery that *The Line, the Cross and the Curve* will later recall.

The dream sequence is often described as the centrepiece of the film, whose surrealist and avant-garde imagery has led to it being acknowledged as a progressive exploration of dance within cinema. Critic Ian Christie comments: 'Before *The Red Shoes*, there were films with dance numbers. After it, there was a new medium which combined dance, design and music in a dreamlike spectacle.'[15] In watching this section of the film, it is not hard to see similarities with the BFS's performances in musical videos which often did the same thing.

The obsessive quality of the red shoes saturates the ambience of Powell and Pressburger's film. As in the original tale, a tension between the exuberant forces of excess and the desire to control them is central. Lermontov, the director of the ballet company, grapples with his position of authority in the face of such intoxication. He hardly ever smiles and is presented as a workaholic who sacrifices intimate personal relationships in the name of art. He also encourages all other members of the company to behave in the same way. Julian Craster, the composer and conductor, carries out his duties with uttermost seriousness.

The importance of discipline and diligence is no better demonstrated than by the dance form that the film glorifies: the art of precise, controlled movement used within ballet. In ballet, with its exact forms and angular but graceful movements, there is a striving for perfection and discipline, ensuring there is no room for mistakes outside of the prescribed steps.

Although Page's commitment to her dancing career is clear, the dramatic 'art or death' option is far more strictly enforced for her than for the male characters. She is subject to a limited set of options that are afforded to women within male-defined cultures. She is compelled to choose between her husband Julian Craster and her dancing career with the ballet Lermontov. She cannot have both because her husband will not allow it, and Lermontov insists on enforcing an either/or non-choice between work and Page's matrimonial life.

Of course, it is not simply dance that Lermontov is forcing Page to choose: his love for her is sublimated into his control of her work (his workaholic nature will not allow him to relate to her in any other way). By the end of the film her husband Julian Craster appears to have lost all sense in his attempts to control her. He abandons the opening night of his opera in London in order to confront Page in Monte Carlo, just before she is to return to her role as the principal dancer in 'The Red Shoes.'

The film does display some ambivalence towards these constrictions, even if it sees no way of transforming them and, ultimately, condemns Page to a tragic death. The options presented are clear: 'Nobody can have two lives and your life is dancing,' Lermontov barks, later commanding Page to leave the company and 'be a faithful housewife.'[16] Lermontov's conviction that she must surrender all other aspects of her life in order to be a world class dancer further emphasises the lack of space Page has to move within her female gendered body. Her husband offers equally limited options, demanding that she abandon her dancing ambitions and sacrifice her career to his will.

Page's body in the story becomes a battleground for the two men's opposing desires to have her at their command. The final scenes demonstrate Page's inability to escape her position as a woman dancer existing at the mercy of male defined social (and storytelling) structures. The final scenes of her life focus on the frantic and unstoppable movement of the red shoes as they dance her to her death, a death which signals escape from the oppressive prison of relationships that surround her. Death here, like many plots which feature women embedded within male-defined stories, is often the only avenue of escape if the woman is to claim a liberated position within a plot structure that denies her any real choices.[17]

The ending of *The Red Shoes* clearly displays sympathy with Page's tragedy at the film's close. The pathos is concentrated in the empty spotlight indicating where she would have been dancing in the ballet's final performance. The red shoes lead Page to fall in front of a train in a dramatic and gory death. The ending of the film recalls the original tale as Craster comes to symbolically occupy the position of executioner, by taking off her red shoes as she lies dying on the railway track.

The BFS's reclamation of the red shoes

Powell and Pressburger's version of *The Red Shoes* provided another arena where artists could interact with the powerful symbolism carried within the red shoes. Their interpretation certainly had an impact on the BFS's versions of the tale; indicated by the inclusion of red ballet shoes for the cover image of the album (nowhere in the original tale does it specify that the shoes are in any way connected to ballet).

The influence of Michael Powell in particular, both in an artistic and personal sense, looms over both works. The song 'Moments of Pleasure' on *The Red Shoes* album, recalls a meeting with Powell 'On a balcony in New York'[18] shortly before he died: 'He meets us at the lift/ Like Douglas Fairbanks/ Waving his walking stick' (RS).

'Moments of Pleasure' has a dreamlike, cinematic quality to it. The sweeping violin sound that envelops the soundscape in the chorus, contrasts with the verse which is accompanied by a minimal piano melody. Inserted into the body of *The Red Shoes* album is an expansive visual landscape. The song pans through the surroundings where the meeting occurred, creating a distinct sense of place, joined to the delicious intoxication of cinema: 'The buildings of New York/ Look just like mountains through the snow' (*RS*).

The song moves between spaces: 'I think about us lying/ Lying on a beach somewhere' (*RS*), as well as particular sites such as the New York cityscape. The 'moments of pleasure' that are articulated, suggest memories cannot be separated from the pain of recalling them. They express acute awareness of 'Just being alive/ It can really hurt' (*RS*). This phrase is an important refrain that is woven through the album.

For women artists in particular, who contribute more and more to the production of culture in the twentieth and twenty-first centuries, the symbol of the red shoes holds a particular attraction. This is due to the curse that surrounds them: wearing the shoes results in a gender-specific death. The challenge presented by the shoes is to inhabit and re-claim them as a positive symbol, to harness them in support of women's creative powers, sustenance and renewal.

This tactic can be partially seen in the 1939 musical film *The Wizard of Oz*. The film presents a typically circumscribed empowerment for women within male-defined cultures, relaying a tactic that will be mirrored by the BFS later on in *The Line, the Cross and the Curve*. In *The Wizard of Oz*, red shoes are harnessed as a source of strength and protection for Dorothy from the wicked witch as the story pitches one woman's power *against* the other woman.

This successful example of where the red shoes are harnessed for personal control is unusual - their symbolism is generally used to signal an undoing of equilibrium. Arguably, other ways the symbolism of *The Line, The Cross and the Curve* allude to *The Wizard of Oz* can be seen by invoking the power of three symbols - brain, heart and courage. These reflect the BFS's rhythmic use of the symbols; line, cross and curve in her version.

Despite the ease with which the shoes are harnessed in *The Wizard of Oz*, reclaiming the shoes is still not an easy task. This is because of the story-telling structure and symbolic possibility of the red shoes as it has developed in the two influential works by Hans Christian Andersen and Powell and Pressburger. These works form the dual core influences for the BFS's *Red Shoes* project.

Powell and Pressburger's version of *The Red Shoes* would have obvious resonance for the BFS. When she began her life she constructed her persona as a dancer as much as a musician and songwriter. Later on in her life she would integrate the role of producer too. The BFS's relationship to expression through movement is arguably unique in the pop world; she presents her art in a holistic manner. All these aspects are important for understanding the work she produces; she invites an understanding of bodily, sonic and visual expressions and how they interplay.

The BFS composes music that was made for her (and others) to dance to. It is fiercely rhythmic and some of her most memorable performances are of her body in motion. Nevertheless, it is her inability to dance smoothly and fluidly that forms the basic plot of *The Line, The Cross and The Curve*. This sets the tone of the rest of the film, which is about lending oneself to the desire for expression. In practice this desire proves too overwhelming to sustain, leading to mania or madness.

The opening song of both album and film, 'Rubberband Girl,' is a plea for elasticity and subtle, responsive movement. The BFS wishes to be 'a rubberband bouncing back to life/ A rubberband bend the beat/ If I could learn to give like a rubberband/ I'd be back on my feet (*RS*).

In the film the BFS is seen dancing in a rehearsal studio. Towards the end her dancing partner places her in a strait jacket (which, of course, mental patients wear) and she swings in it tortuously, from side to side. Here the BFS performs the role of 'mad woman' that popular culture, all too often, set out for her. This imagery is also suggestive of the strait jacket of 'The Red Shoes' story itself, with its limited space for the female character to move within.

Even the sounds used in 'Rubberband Girl' betray the existence of male-defined musical codes. The climax is populated by electric guitar solos and tenor saxophones. The combination of these sounds communicates culturally naturalised ideas of male-defined genius. These are represented by the phallic guitar, while the deep noises made by the saxophone signify masculine musical prowess and presence enclosing upon the BFS's artful frustrations. The BFS does not concede her territory completely. She abandons coherent language by vocally mimicking the texture of a rubber band, before invoking the domestic imagery of washing up, 'rub-a-dub-a-dub-dub' (*RS*), as a form of resistance.

Nevertheless, the BFS exhaustedly submits to the cultural codes that would define her as mad. In acts of revelry she reaffirms their ridicule which highlights awareness of such stereotypical perceptions of her in culture. This is a dangerous tactic to engage with as it reinforces a damaging stereotype even as she deconstructs it. Here the BFS's grappling with the symbolic possibility of *The Red Shoes* yields little more success than for Karen in the original tale, or for Page in Powell and Pressburger's film. The BFS's engagement with 'The Red Shoes' is carried out in order to test its limits although she finds it hard to move beyond those limits.

The BFS and fairytale therapy

In his study *The Uses of Enchantment* (1976), Bruno Bettleheim describes the fairy tale as having an important part to play in a child's personal development.[19] He suggests fairy tales offer a therapeutic function for a person 'through contemplating what the story seems to imply about him and his inner conflicts at this moment in his life.'[20] This description of the use of the fairy tale is an appropriate way to understand the BFS's engagement with *The Red Shoes*.

According to Bettleheim's theory, the fairy tale provides ways to help a person work through problems at a moment of crisis. If we are to diagnose the BFS in a therapeutic sense at this time in her life, we could argue the crisis she faces is a creative one. After having been a prolific creative being for many years, she is now suffering from the challenge she set for herself to continuously invent new forms of life. To put it simply, the BFS in *The Red Shoes* is burnt out. Turning to the fairy tale form is one of the many avenues she uses to help her work through these creative and personal difficulties. Ritual magic and occult practices are also drawn upon, and will be explored later in this chapter.

The red shoes that the BFS wears on *The Line, the Cross and the Curve* are ballet shoes, but she does not solely dance ballet steps in them. She struggles, in fact, to dance en pointe. The shoes pull her forcefully in the directions *they* choose to move, while her all-black heavy clothing accentuates the clumsiness of her steps. As she breaks through a mirror, a classic surrealist avenue to the Underworld, the music of 'The Red Shoes' explodes portentously, sung by the male voices that are familiar tones in the BFS's soundscapes: 'She gotta dance, she gotta dance/ And she can't stop 'till them shoes come off/ These shoes do, a kind of voodoo,/ They're gonna make her dance 'till her legs fall off' (*RS*).

The BFS is enticed through the mirror by the shoemaker, played by Lindsey Kemp, her dance tutor in the late 70s. On the other side of the mirror she is seen in a new costume, a more sexualised red and black dress, as she tears through the Underworld accompanied by streams of colourful ribbons, joined by the shoemaker who is her menacing guide. He is painted in similar white facial make-up to the parallel character in Powell and Pressburger's film - another way *The Line, the Cross and the Curve* recycles the imagery of their version.

The shoemaker and the BFS dance with one another and alone, engaging with a variety of different dance forms. The majority of these do not correspond to ballet steps. They are seen doing jive dancing and basic contact moves and parodies of Irish dancing. Then the camera focuses on the graceful movements of the shoes themselves prior to the BFS's exhausted collapse in the arms of the shoemaker.

It is the significant that the BFS dances non-ballet steps in ballet shoes. It points to the uncontrollable power of the red shoes while also demonstrating how the BFS breaks the constraints of the ballet tradition. On behalf of the spectator, ballet has traditionally invited detached ways of viewing the dance. Roger Copeland writes: 'Balletic turnout promotes *the goal of visibility*, opening the body up so that it becomes theatrically legible when framed by a proscenium arch.'[21]

A dance form geared toward detached spectatorship is largely at odds with the type of dance performances that can be found not only in *The Line, the Cross and the Curve*, but throughout the BFS's career. The BFS's dance performances often embroil viewers into the scene of the dance, nurturing moments of exchange between bodies and senses. The BFS tramples indiscreetly and fervently in the red ballet shoes, she will not be contained within their rigid steps. Her arms and legs flail, moving in indiscriminate directions, creating new spaces that have not yet been invented. The BFS's possession by the shoes does not mean she has no power to dismember the ballet form. She does this as she moves within them.

Interventions: symbols and voice

The title of *The Line, the Cross and the Curve* already displays a desire to break with simple re-writings of 'The Red Shoes.' It is taken from invented symbols that are used to rewrite the destiny of an unnamed female character who finds herself embedded in the story of the red shoes: 'this curve, is your smile/ And this cross, is your heart/ And this line, is your path' (*RS*).

These three symbols are suggestive of equilibrium and direction. These are important qualities that elude the girl in the original tale, as her personal control is displaced through the possession imposed by the spell of the red shoes.

In *The Line, the Cross and the Curve*, the BFS attempts to transform the symbolic universe of the tale. She extends the terrain of symbols away from the singular symbolic power of the red shoes. This offers a *potential* exit from the inevitability of the story that usually results in hopeless suicide. This enables the BFS to address the insufficiencies of the original, while reusing the tale and its retelling in the 1948 film as a basis for a new interpretation.

The most striking and positive aspect of BFS's reclamation of the red shoes, is in the areas where she gives power to the female character to shape her destiny. At worst 'The Red Shoes' celebrates the extreme punishment for the self-desiring mobile woman. At best it presents sympathy, as seen in the powerful tragedy depicted at the end of the Powell and Pressburger film. Through this claiming of power we see the BFS in action as she reworks the story.

Apart from Anne Sexton's poem 'The Red Shoes,' which also identifies with the suicidal tendencies embedded in the red shoes,[22] *The Red Shoes* and *The Line, the Cross and the Curve* are significant because as a woman, the BFS *chooses* to wear the shoes and place herself in its story. She claims the red shoes as a powerful statement of her autonomy over the forces that destroy the girls in previous versions of the tale. She is writer, producer, dancer and musician of the music, text and movement. As we will see, this reclamation works on a number of levels within the tale and with varying degrees of success.

Critic Bonnie Gordon suggests that the BFS's 'technological proficiency is part of what allows her to rewrite "The Red Shoes." With it [she] exhibits mastery and control, precisely what the fairy tale takes away from its protagonist.'[23] It is not just the BFS's ability in the recording studio that enables her to rewrite this tale. It is a combination of all her skills as musical and visual artist, and an awareness of how patriarchal story-telling structures marginalise women and prevent them from telling their story in their own voice.

Gordon suggests the BFS uses her multiplicity to resist the story of 'The Red Shoes.' The song 'The Red Shoes' has 'multiple meanings and multiple voices. [...] [The] plurality of voices, the endless repetition of the song that defies closure, and the sometimes dissonant meanings resist a fixed interpretation.'[24] The song, like the shoes, refuses to settle into an easy conclusive space. It opens up possibility for alternatives and invites multiple engagements and interpretations.

In both the album and the film, the song 'The Red Shoes' functions as the centre-piece. It appears literally in the middle of *The Red Shoes* album while in *The Line, the Cross and the Curve* it acts as a refrain and motif throughout. The song presents a dialogue between the current owner of the shoes, and the desiring girl (played by the BFS), who admires the shoes. When she sees them on another woman, she dreams of being able to dance as well as she can: 'Oh she move like the Diva do/ I said "I'd like to dance like you"' (*RS*).

Already this marks a divergence from the original tale, as it is a *woman* who hands over the shoes, escaping their spell in the process. While this does not alter the endurance of the red shoes, the unnamed woman character does break away from the curse through the extended symbols of the line, cross and curve.

'The Red Shoes' dramatises the intense moment in performance where dreams and fantasies become realised in fairy-tale scenarios: 'Oh it's gonna be the way you always thought it would be/ But it's gonna be no illusion/ Oh it's gonna be the way you always dreamt about it/ But it's gonna be really happening to ya' (*RS*). The 'dream come true' of becoming a good dancer is turning into a nightmare as dance is expressed as a form of madness. The BFS's dream is granted fulfilment, but as in the original tale, it carries with it punishment.

In *The Line, the Cross and the Curve* the BFS breaks through the mirror in the dance rehearsal studio. This rewrites the mirror imagery of Powell and Pressburger's film where Page, performing the part of Karen, dances before a shop window. In their film the window can only reflect her desire for the shoes and the gratuitous vanity they symbolise. For the BFS, the other side of the mirror leads to the spiritual and mental challenge presented by the Underworld. It is also where the punishment takes hold as the shoes thoroughly possess her.

This Underworld space also demonstrates an affinity with Cocteau's surrealist film *The Blood of the Poet* (1930). In Cocteau's film, he is seen jumping through a mirror that is a gateway to an Underworld of surreal events which contort time and space. The BFS's journey into the Underworld similarly works within a fantastical time frame as she undergoes a series of psychic and spiritual challenges.

The importance of the Underworld scenes in *The Line, the Cross and the Curve* should be understood in light of the writer Joseph Campbell and his work on comparative mythology.[25] From the 1940s onwards,

Campbell researched and wrote about the unifying themes in myth and tales across Western and Eastern cultures. Along with Carl Jung, he 'attested to the tremendous power of myth in the collective unconscious of humanity' and suggested that 'without myth, we are cut off from our spiritual roots.'[26] Campbell advocated the study of comparative mythology as an avenue through which human beings, as part of a collective community, can connect with the meaning of life.

The mythic aspects of the BFS's versions of *The Red Shoes* are of great importance. *The Line, the Cross and the Curve* sees the BFS engage with archetypal mythic activities. In particular, her voyage into the Underworld 'is but one of innumerable such adventures undertaken by the heroes of fairy tale and myth.'[27] Campbell suggested this voyage is one of the core activities the hero must undertake within mythological stories.

The BFS's reclamation of the story also provides the Karen character with a narrative voice. This was not present in other versions of the story. In the original tale, our relationship to Karen is framed by male-defined, Christian judgements. This is heightened by the distance of the narrator's third-person perspective which tells the story. The BFS on the other hand gives voice to the possessed girl who wears the shoes.

The most important scene in the film is the monologue that details the unstoppable days and nights of dancing that occur when the shoes take hold:

> In these shoes every step I take is laced with madness. They fill me with pain and confusion, with thoughts that are not my own. I have danced their dances. I see streets and buildings I know so well although I have never been to these places. *Together we raced* with wild horses until they dropped, we have leapt from cliffs into the raging waters below and *together we tripped* from a stage into a pit. I see me falling, I feel my fear and yet I was never here. These shoes are all anger and passion. I am possessed and no longer have the strength to fight them.[28]

For the first time the tale's audience gains a sympathetic insight into the experience of what it is like to *wear* the red shoes. The experience of madness, pain and confusion is clearly communicated; they are not merely a justified punishment for vanity. As in the original tale the shoes have a personality of their own. They are the demented dancing partner who refuses to rest. Highlighting the shoes' possessive powers clearly recalls the original tale. It was also important for Powell and Pressburger who use the night-time dancing sequence in the ballet performance as an imaginative exploration of both Karen and Page's worlds, as these two experiences appear to cross over.

Ritual reclamation and the search for alternative meaning

The layers of meaning in *The Red Shoes* and T*he Line, the Cross and the Curve* are multiple. Both are deeply saturated with references to spirituality and healing. They carry a deep preoccupation with symbols, rituals and magick as avenues for salvation and healing. Do the spiritual universes explored on *The Red Shoes* offer ways to escape the spell of the shoes? How does an understanding of ritual and magick give us further insight into the challenge the BFS is making to the story?

Spirituality and healing have always played an important part in the life of the BFS. She displayed an interest in the occult from early on in her life, exploring non-western philosophical and spiritual traditions on *The Kick Inside* and *The Dreaming*. In *The Line, the Cross and the Curve* the BFS presents herself in an explicitly witchy manner. After the tortuous dancing of 'Rubberband Girl' we encounter the BFS alone. She is dressed in black, surrounded by candles in her music room as she sings 'It Must Be Love.' The eeriness of the scene is accentuated by the lack of electricity. This gives the room, lit only by a solitary candle and flashes of lightning, an archaic feeling. The BFS's magick and deviance is connected to her ability to compose music. Viewers are encouraged to note the musical score sheets that are scattered about her room.

This scene also features a blackbird, an animal the BFS refers to in 'Waking the Witch' from *Hounds of Love* (1985) which connects the bird to witches: 'The blackbird/ Wings in the water – go down.../ "She's a witch"/ (Help this blackbird, there's a stone around my leg).[29] In folklore blackbirds are often seen as symbols of darkness, sin and the temptations of the flesh.[30] 'And So Is Love' shows the BFS tenderly holding a blackbird before she releases it into the room, where it flies into a window and dies. The BFS then picks up the bird (who lands on her music) and places it upon some red velvet fabric, kissing it as she does so. Here she displays her mourning for a bird that is symbolically seen as dangerous, and aligns herself with it. Blackbirds are evocative of a witchlike presence in the BFS's own mythological universe. I will return to this point in the final chapter of the book.

In the film's next scene, the unnamed female character breaks the BFS's solitude as she runs through the mirror from the Underworld. She is presumably drawn to her because she has particular powers. The BFS easily takes up the challenge she presents to her: drawing three symbols on a piece of a paper that will break the spell of the red shoes and enable the girl to return home. Their interaction on film suggests the BFS has a previous familiarity with magick. The paper flies into the hands of the doomed lady in a seemingly magickal way and viewers are encouraged to note the occurrence of a spell.

As the BFS is transported to the Underworld, her appearance is evidence of her heretical behaviour. This further underlines how she deviates from the Christian moral values that form the basis of the original tale. In the Underworld she is plastered with starkly contrasting white and red make-up on her face. She writhes and dances in demonic ecstasy through the fire.

Spirituality and divination are central to the process of redemption explored in the Underworld. Unlike Karen in the original tale, the BFS is able to harness these spiritual powers for instruction, guidance and protection. This is completely opposite to the original tale where spirituality and religion are used to prolong punishment and confer judgement upon her bodily and spiritual 'sin.'

The appearance of Bush's real-life healer Lily in the song 'Lily,' is a pivotal moment in the healing process depicted within the film. The prayer Lily utters includes lines from Starhawk's 'Charge of the Goddess' (1979) - 'From me all things proceed and unto me they must return'[31] - as the BFS's clings to her body in a desperate fashion, communicating her emotional and spiritual turmoil. Through Lily a healing ritual is initiated. The ritual will be recognised by practitioners of classic Kabbalah as the Lesser Banishing Ritual of the Pentagram. As Nevill Drury explains:

> in ceremonial magic [it is] a ritual designed to ward off negative and evil influences. The banishing ritual of the Lesser Pentagram is performed in a magical circle and commences in the East. The magician uses a sword to inscribe pentagrams in the air and invokes the archangels Raphael, Gabriel, Michael, and Uriel at the four quarters. The banishing also includes a ritual Prayer known as the "Kabbalistic Cross."[32]

Both the song and film directly reference this ritual practice: from the song we hear the invocation, while in the film the angels rise in their quarters as a circle of fire is drawn, creating a sacred and protected space around the BFS. Here an important piece of ritual magic is placed at the centre of 'Lily.' It re-enacts ritualistic practices every time the song is listened to: 'Gabriel before me/ Raphael behind me/ Michael to my right/ Uriel on my left side' (*RS*).

The invocation of the archangels directly connects the ritual with the Kabbalistic Tree of Life, as each angel rules a quarter that corresponds to an element and direction: Gabriel (West, Water); Raphael (East, Air); Michael (South, Fire) and Uriel (North, Earth).[33] According to Dion Fortune, this ritual can be used for a number of things: to protect against psychic attack, to purify or clear a room before a ritual and to aid meditation by promoting a clear mind free from outside influences.[34] In the film it seems to be working on all of these levels. The ritual acts as an avenue to reclaim personal power within the tale, warding off the spell imposed upon the BFS. 'This is my space' (*RS*) she sings, redrawing her boundaries in a protective manner.

This ritual creates a crucial site where the power of the BFS is replenished. As Carol Christ argues: 'rituals enhance the power of symbols because they involve the body, the source of our deepest feeling'. They speak to the 'conscious and unconscious mind, uniting rational awareness with our deepest non-rational knowledge.'[35] In other words, rituals work in an embodied and emotional manner. They break down dualisms and unite forms of understanding usually placed in opposition to one another (such as rational and irrational, mind and body, reason and emotion, which we saw the BFS deconstruct through her breakdown on 'Sat in Your Lap'). They do not transcend these systems but work *within* them. They re-order the social and sacred universe, creating a culture with a different mythos where 'new values and new ways of living are made possible.'[36] Dion Fortune further elaborates:

> The Qabalists [...] do not try to explain to the mind that which the mind is not equipped to deal with; they give it a series of symbols to meditate upon, and these enable it to build the stairway of realisation step by step and to climb where it cannot fly. [37]

Deploying symbols creates a series of alternative co-ordinates from which to understand phenomena. This system operates on a different level to the rational mind which cannot 'fly' to these realms. This opens up possibilities for understanding the function of symbols in *The Line, the Cross and the Curve*. Consequently, the use of ritual, magick and symbols in the film fragments the power of the story's traditional symbology which is based on a symbolic system that encases women and punishes their desire for autonomy, self-desire and movement. It is a punishment symbolised and held within the red shoes.

Following the Kabbalistic ritual in the film, the BFS is seen falling into a meditative space. The ritual strengthens her in the fight to reverse the power of the spell of the line, the cross and the curve. In the song 'Moments of Pleasure' she is asked to 'call upon those she loves' (*RS*). This highlights the importance of memorialising as a source of meditative love and power. The BFS is then seen floating in a pre-heavenly space as she remembers people who have left the mortal realm. This space acts as the indeterminate arena where contact and crossing can occur between worlds. She rotates, encircled by the people she remembers as they pass through and between realms. Amongst them is a reference to Bush's mother, Hannah, who died during the making of the album: 'And I can hear my mother saying/ "Every old sock meets an old shoe"/ isn't that a great saying?' (*RS*).

The heavy emphasis on the spiritual that pervades the works may have emerged as a response to mourning. If we remember that in the original tale Karen's initial violation with the shoes was framed as an inappropriate response to her mother's death, and Bettleheim's point that most fairy tales begin with the death of a mother or father,[38] then the red shoes tale provides a suitable arena in which to explore the experience of grief and maternal mourning.

The spiritual universe of *The Red Shoes* draws on Irish Catholic iconography. This is taken from Bush's mother's lineage. It is in this healing and concluding space that the process of 'becoming Irish' that began on *The Dreaming* is played out. After *The Dreaming* the BFS coloured her musical paths with more Irish inflections. Both *Hounds of Love* and *The Sensual World* draw upon such traditions, from the infectious 'Jig of Life' to 'The Sensual World' itself.

This 'Irish turn' in her life is found in the mystical fabric of *The Red Shoes*. It is embedded within the layers of mysticism and grief that are integral to album and film. The entwining of these forces are powerfully expressed in 'Big Stripey Lie': 'Your name is being called by sacred things/ That are not addressed nor listened to/ Sometimes they blow trumpets' (*RS*).

The references throughout the album to the sacred heart of Jesus emerge from Catholic iconography. This is a form of devotion used in the Catholic Church to represent the divine love for humanity. 'Why Should I Love You,' which begins with the trio Bulgarka singing a religious eulogy and features remixes and vocals by pop superstar Prince, feeds into this tradition. It is an extended hymn of devotion to the iconography embodied by the sacred heart, done of course, in the BFS's own style: 'Have you ever seen a picture/ Of Jesus laughing?/ *Mmm*, do you think/ He had a beautiful smile?' (*RS*, italics mine).

The BFS's 'Mmm' is evocative of her previous use of the phrase in the 1989 song 'The Sensual World.' Here she took the phrase from Molly Bloom's soliloquy in Joyce's *Ulysses*. The BFS commented that she used the 'Mmm' to 'express myself as a female in a female way and I found that original piece (Molly Bloom's speech) very female talking.'[39] It is used again in this song to conjure the same aspects of sensuality.

Engaging with a Catholic doctrine that harbours conservative ideas about gender and sexuality is not without its restrictions. However, the BFS's exploration of the devotional imagery of Jesus in relation to ideas about love and healing is foundational for *The Red Shoes*. To counter the severity of Catholic doctrine the BFS places her own particular emphasis on religious images and ideas. These brim with embodied feminine sensuality: 'The red of the Sacred Heart/ The grey of a ghost,' while 'the 'L' of the lips are open/ The 'O' of the Host/ The 'V' of the Velvet (*RS*). Here the BFS (and Prince) evoke a specifically female divine presence. The open velvet lips that host the sacred heart are suggestive of the vagina. This is connected to love - the 'E of my eye/ The eye of wonder' (*RS*) - which articulates a positive perception of the world, spirituality, body and soul.

Merging the grey 'ghost' of the Holy Spirit with suggestions of sexual openness provides a physical and spiritual map that runs counter to male-defined religious iconography. This splits the spirit from the body and sees fleshiness as a sign of damnation, rather than sacredness. By reconfiguring and perverting traditional iconography, the BFS establishes an embodied and divined sexuality in *The Red Shoes*. This is a knowledge suppressed and forbidden within the dominant, male-defined religions.

Constructing a genealogy of female-centred divinity is, for Irigaray, an essential part of a culture that recognises female sexual difference.

The BFS has drawn upon such a genealogy, as well as constructing it throughout her life. At various stages this was more important than others: you will remember her early life was fascinated by the mysteries of menstruation and other 'strange phenomena.' It has always been there in some form though, propelling her movement.

Irigaray argues that recognising difference *through* divinity must be achieved before culture can move beyond dualistic, male-dominated frameworks into a society of radical sexual difference. This will then lead to respect for multiple differences:

> Divinity is what we need to become free, autonomous, sovereign. No human subjectivity, no human society has ever been established without the help of the divine. There comes a time for destruction, but before destruction is possible, Gods of the gods must exist [...] our theological tradition presents some difficulty as far as God in the feminine gender is concerned. There is no *woman* God, no female trinity: mother, daughter and spirit.[40]

Much of the BFS's work as an artist is about asserting an experience of feminine divinity within popular song and music video. She presents a way of being that celebrates the immanent divinity of the self-defined female subject, her sexuality and creativity.

The BFS's portrayal of divinity emerges from her figuration of immanent female sexual power and agency. 'The Song of Solomon' rewrites one of the most sexually explicit parts of the bible, and plainly voices female sexual demands: 'Don't want your bullshit, yeah/ Just want your sexuality' (*RS*). This is coupled with hyperbolic romanticism: 'I'll come in a hurricane for you/ I'll do it for you' (*RS*). This song further links it with witchcraft through the text *The Key of Solomon: a Grimoire*, which was a major influence on the religion.

On *The Red Shoes* and *The Line, the Cross and the Curve*, the BFS creates a cultural framework where embodied, emotional and spiritual intelligence can flourish. This radically challenges humanist, male-defined culture which denies and suppresses the body, emotion and their relation to spirit. The BFS's adventures in *The Red Shoes* help to break the symbolic spell of that system. She offers a symbolic intervention that unites the rational and the irrational, the body and the spirit within an experience of the divine that is of 'this world.' This breaks with the prevalence of dualistic, binary understandings, offering an alternative map of the social, cultural and spiritual universe.

The Red Shoes and *The Line, the Cross and the Curve* reference a vast range of magickal, ritualistic, devotional and spiritual systems. These are channelled to protect, heal, celebrate and memorialise the dead. They draw upon Irish mystical and familial ancestry as well as harnessing feminine divine power. To practitioners of ritual magick, the BFS's work on the album will undoubtedly resonate at a deeper level.

Ultimately, the BFS combines spirituality and love as essential qualities which can be harnessed to ensure survival within the confusing state of mortality presented to us: 'Steer your life by these stars/ On the unconditional chance/ 'Tis where hell and heaven dance/ This is the constellation of the heart' (*RS*).

Both the film and the album grapple with the distinction between the material and spiritual worlds - in-between life and death - and often refuse their separation. They display an interpenetration of these realms, blurring the boundaries and celebrating their crossing.

How far does the BFS reclaim her power?

At a linguistic, structural and symbolic level, the BFS's occupation of The Red Shoes story carries with it important changes, but how many of the original story-telling structures remain intact? *The Line, the Cross and the Curve* suggests that women may never be released from the tyranny of the red shoes; they can only be passed like a baton onto other unfortunate, sinning subjects. The final scenes of the film dramatise the BFS's escape from the shoes, as she manages to successfully sing back the symbols (the line, the cross and the curve) and break the spell.

Unfortunately, this is at the expense of the unnamed woman character who tricked her into putting the shoes on in the first place, as she is forced to put them on again. The final scene of the film shows the red shoes writhing above a pile of rubble, refusing to stay still on the legs of their previous owner. This image is suggestive of the power of the red shoes to endure the effects of time, space and multiple realities. The shoes triumph over the BFS's attempts to reduce their symbolic, mythological and narrative power over women's bodies.

The two figures played by Miranda Richardson and Lindsey Kemp are the eternal characters in the story of 'The Red Shoes' – the shoemaker and the girl. It seems the story cannot escape their sovereignty despite the BFS's attempt at reclamation. In this sense the BFS offers only a partial intervention into the story, as the only woman she can save is herself. The other woman is handed a fate of endless punishing movement. This is a classically circumscribed liberation for women within male-defined cultures, which can only be achieved at the expense of another woman.

Ultimately, our final impressions in both the album and the film are of the red shoes. This is indicated particularly by their occupation of the central space on the cover of the album, encouraging us to remain focussed on their symbolic power. They frame the album and the film with a promise that their significance will not be given up easily. Red shoes will not go away without genuine change to the symbolic universe where the story has survived constant retellings for over 150 years. Consequently, the shoes and what they represent will continue to circulate in a damaging way for women - despite the BFS's efforts.

The BFS and the girlish feminine

In her early life, the BFS revelled in the girlish feminine and she celebrated this with her voice. *Lionheart* in particular occupied a number of exceptionally high-pitched spaces. In the BFS's life, the use of high-pitched vocals can be connected to a wilful, imaginative, ingenuous and girlish feminine persona. Such a vocal style is used on *The Red Shoes* and suggests a return to the girlish feminine within the life of the BFS.

On albums leading up to *The Red Shoes*, the BFS displayed a wider vocal range. This spanned the middle and lower registers as well as visceral grunts and noises. These styles marked a departure towards more mature and experimental styles respectively. In returning to the more high-pitched spaces of her vocal range the BFS conjures again this feeling of girlishness in her work. In using the term 'girlishness,' I am not suggesting this displays immaturity or a lack of sophistication. In fact the BFS utilises these vocal registers as spaces of resistance. She shatters taboos by letting these girl voices articulate sexuality and wonder.

In Western society the autonomous voices and desires of young girls are rarely, if ever, heard. This makes the BFS's retelling of stories in a girlish voice particularly challenging and important. In *The Red Shoes* the BFS pitches her vocal solidarity firmly alongside Karen's and other punished girls' lost voices.

The Red Shoes album begins in the high-pitched soprano style of 'Rubberband Girl.' This later gets pulled into a deeper voice by a wrapping bass sound that evokes the bending of a rubber band. In the song 'The Red Shoes' the BFS uses the differences in vocal timbre to occupy the different characters of the story. Importantly, when she occupies the position of the girl she sings in a vibrato soprano before shifting her register lower in order to mark a movement to a different narrative voice. This is something Gordon explores in her article, 'Kate Bush's Subversive Shoes.'[41]

The high vocal style that dominates the work is suggestive of a voice able to carry memory. Such a form of enunciation has the power to trigger associations, at both a personal and collective level. The BFS's vocal style has a unique fluidity and flexibility that can move across time. She can offer a wide range of recognisable female or feminine subjectivities in her voice. The girl voice is particularly appropriate too for the re-articulation of a fairy tale. Fairy tales are something people are introduced to as children – despite their often barbaric nature – and the use of the voice creates an opportunity to move back into that childhood space.

Topically too, the album functions as a vantage point from which to survey the past. This incorporates perspectives and emotions that run throughout the whole of the BFS's life. This retrospective, confessional aspect of the album often expresses weary sentiments. It can be contrasted with her earlier works that often articulated an 'adult' sexuality through the voice of the girl or child: 'We used to say/ "Ah hell, we're young"/ But now we see that life is sad/ And so is love' (*RS*).

The Red Shoes and *The Line, the Cross and the Curve* can be seen as the BFS's most directly confessional work to that date. These confessions emerge between the fabric of old tales, mysticism and spirituality woven into the layers of meaning. The notion of the confessional is doubly ironic, given the divine Catholic presence in the albums.

The inside cover art of *The Red Shoes* encourages people to split themselves open like a variety of fruit, as seeds and juice spill from the insides. The image is sticky, juicy and sexual. There is much emphasis on exploring the 'inside' emotional space on *The Red Shoes*. 'Eat the Music' revels in gorging, splitting, penetrating and celebrating the power of the queer feminine, the BFS sings: 'He's a woman at heart/ And I love him for that/ Let's split him open' (*RS*) multiple 'like a pomegranate/ Insides out/ All is revealed/ Not only women bleed' (*RS*).

The song presents the destruction and merging of boundaries between inside and outside. The BFS feminises masculine sexuality, infusing it with a sensuality, openness, bodily energy and multiplicity. The BFS often presents fluid gender and sexual identities. Here her versions are unique; they foreground feminine power and energy, presenting it as a quality both women and men can possess.

'Eat the Music' also contains the final challenge that the BFS poses to the symbolic logic of the red shoes story. 'Eat the Music' is part of the closing scenes of *The Line, the Cross and the Curve*. In the film, the austere logic of Andersen's Christian morality tale is evoked by the frozen landscape which the BFS falls exhausted upon. Here she is confronted with the unnamed lady who tells her she has to sing back the symbols – line, cross and curve – in order to break the spell. The pair runs through winter into autumn, singing the words to 'Eat the Music': 'split me open/ with devotion' (*RS*). Finally they find themselves in the warmth of summer, represented by a room full of exotic fruits – bananas, pa-

payas, guavas and many more - where the BFS is impelled to 'Eat the Music' in a final, ecstatic dance.

This scene *should* be read for its dubious racial imagery and the way it bluntly exoticises blackness, and perpetuates racialised stereotypes to do with voodoo. For the room is also full of black bodies surrounded by an abundance of fruit whose bursting seeds, juices and flesh sexualise them. The BFS's position as the only white person in the room accentuates this.

You will recall from the video for 'Sat in Your Lap' the BFS similarly plays black against white in a visual interpretation of her song. In this case however, she doesn't destabilise racialised codes at all, but reinforces sexualised fantasies of exotic blackness which abound in the white supremacist imaginaries. These fantasies are wholly part of the racist power structures that the BFS, as a white woman, benefits from, perpetuates, and here glorifies. The music also runs close to cultural appropriation with its Madagascan rhythm and sound.

In the context of the spiritual codes within the film though (the space where the BFS finds most resistance to 'The Red Shoes' story), blackness is associated with the warmth that melts the icy spell cast over the BFS. She is seen to undergo a process of positive repossession of the 'shoes [that] do/ a kind of voodoo' (*RS*). This filters heat and love into her body so that she can carry through to fight in the final stages of the film.

The BFS is placed in the middle of the room as a shaman figure places his hand above her head, forcing it to move in hypnotic, circular motions. As the BFS – complete with tribal red streaks brushed across her face - enters into a trance, the healer further shakes his hands around the energy fields of her body, releasing the rhythms of the spell's possession.

Finally the spell is broken as the BFS's smile, heart and path fly back to her on the original pieces of paper, while the unnamed woman chases after them in vain. As she awakes the shoes are no longer on her feet. They are returned to their original owner. In this final scene, the BFS aligns herself with the powers of blackness that enables her to escape the spell cast by the cold, white, Christian morality tale. The symbolic codes the BFS uses in the story underwrite the logic and cold frigidity of whiteness that consistently punish women for their desire to move. Instead the warmth ushers forth a fluidity that creates greater flexibility and movement – symbolic, physical and spiritual.

Ultimately though, the red shoes remain a symbol of the BFS's creative exhaustion. Despite her escape in the film from the spell, her possession by her art, and her surrender to it she makes known by wearing the red shoes, the shoes endure as the lasting symbol in the story. *The Red Shoes* is all about submission and defeat. We see the BFS wave a white flag. She can no longer sustain her level of creativity and productivity that characterised her early life. She needs to rest. As she commented at the time, she had been possessed by her work and must now take control back:

> the image of dance... is something I've really enjoyed being involved in. But it's an image you can take to almost any form of art, the idea of being possessed by one's art. Sometimes *it* controls you rather than *you* controlling it.[42]

In this chapter we have seen the BFS commit suicide by choosing to wear the red shoes. She has attempted to negotiate the story-telling structures of 'The Red Shoes' story but ultimately cannot overcome their symbolic power. We have seen the strong re-emergence of spirituality as an important facet in her life. This will be continued in the final chapter of the journey as we explore the importance of rebirth as a fundamental power of the BFS. Rebirth enables the BFS to escape the death she chose for herself. Onto the final stages of her life: the rebirth and disappearance of the BFS.

The rebirth of the BFS

We are now reaching the end of our journey with the BFS, although there are still some moves we need to make. In this book the BFS has danced, sung and taken on many different shapes and sizes. Chapter one witnessed her powerful birth through the female body. She extolled the virtues of menstruation, and celebrated the divinity of herself and the earth as a whole.

Chapter two was all about performance. The BFS camped it up in order to find ways she could express herself and her fascination with sexuality. At the same time as being a vanguard in relation to gender and sexuality, this chapter demonstrated how the BFS reinforced stereotypical ideas about race, Englishness and whiteness.

Chapter three contained the dramatic breakdown of the BFS, as life as she knew it fell radically apart. This breakdown was also a breakthrough: it was the shift she needed to help her explore new connections with the world. In chapter four we saw the death of the BFS. Wearing red shoes as a symbol of her suicide, these works were about her abandonment to her art - a death that meant she would not be seen in public for another twelve years.

Within the lifespan of the BFS (1978 -) death will always be birth. In the final part of the BFS's journey, I will return to her most important quality: rebirth. You will remember from chapter one how the theme of rebirth was introduced early in the BFS's life, in the song 'Room for Life' from *The Kick Inside*. Since then rebirth has been a central force generating the multiple lives of the BFS. Rebirth allows the BFS to be powerful, creative and energetic. It makes her resilient - she can survive death over and over again. Her ability to be reborn makes her life a sustainable project.

To fully explore the importance of rebirth in the BFS's life, we need to move backwards in time to the song-suite 'The Ninth Wave' from *Hounds of Love* (1985). We will then finish our time with the BFS by exploring the rebirth journey on 'A Sky of Honey' from the 2005 album *Aerial*. This will mark the final disappearance of the BFS, a disappearance that 'escapes'[1] subjectivity itself.

'The Ninth Wave' as a Rebirth Journey

Hounds of Love stands out for critics and fans as Bush's most fully realised piece of work.[2] It offers a balance of the experimental and the popular, while still managing to appeal to a wide audience. It has been described by Moy as a '"seminal text" in popular music.'[3] It also contains an extended meditation on the concept of rebirth.

Rebirth is alluded to thematically in various forms throughout the BFS's life. Created through the maternal body, the BFS's languages of dying consistently become an avenue from which she articulates transformation. Death helps her negotiate subjectivity, casting off old selves and embracing new ones: 'Suddenly there in the road,/ Is your old self,/ Trying to get out of the rain' ('Fullhouse,' *LH*). 'All the Love' from *The Dreaming* suggests these deaths are multiple: 'the first time I died,/ was in the arms of good friends of mine' (*TD*). The cycles of death and birth everywhere animate the BFS's life.

It is on 'The Ninth Wave' that the conceptual exploration of rebirth is most fully realised. 'The Ninth Wave' dramatises a journey through extreme crisis that, if survived, will ultimately lead to greater wisdom and strength. In a journey that prefigures the movement into the Underworld in *The Line, the Cross and the Curve*, 'The Ninth Wave' can be read as a more acute exploration of this ancient, mythological and shamanic journey. It is also consistent with the BFS's interest in spiritual systems and modes of healing.

Stanislav Grof describes the shamanic journey as follows:

> An ancient spiritual system and healing art intimately connected [...] with death and dying. The career of many shamans begins with the 'shamanic illness,' a spontaneous initiatory crisis involving a visionary journey into the Underworld, experience of psychological death and rebirth, and ascent into supernal realms. The knowledge of the realm of death acquired during this transformation makes it possible for the shaman to move freely back and forth between the two worlds and use these journeys for healing purposes and for obtaining knowledge. He or she can also mediate such journeys for others.[4]

In many ways 'The Ninth Wave' follows such a pattern. The crisis the BFS undergoes seems to be spontaneous, and it certainly harnesses visionary powers. The journey of 'The Ninth Wave' is also intensely preoccupied with death, dying and rebirth. The number of the title carries symbolic significance because it refers to the nine months in which a woman carries a child inside her.

The song-suite offers listeners a trial of endurance. As a journey it crosses a large number of psychic states and situations. These challenges must be overcome in order to reach a new state of knowledge.

In the Underworld of 'The Ninth Wave' the challenge the BFS needs to integrate has important gendered historical dimensions. She is forced to confront woman's demonised cultural history. This is represented by the witch who appears in the middle of the song-suite. Diane Purkiss has written how the figure of the witch has been 'constantly recast as the late twentieth century's idea of a proto-feminist, a sister from the past'[5] who operates as a site of 'identification and elaborate fantasy'[6] for women artists.

The BFS affirms such identifications. She uses the witch as a symbol of women's autoerotic desire and independent power. This is a central point that I have made about the BFS's life – she celebrates a desire independent of male identification, a desire for herself and for others. The figure of the witch has been used by feminist writers in a similar way. She helps to assert independent female sexuality since 'female eroticism is terrifying; it is an earthquake, a volcanic eruption, a tidal wave.'[7]

Focussing on the figure of the witch on 'The Ninth Wave' helps further understandings of how the BFS creates myths to reclaim autonomous female sexuality. Before moving on to the encounter with the witch herself – which forms the centrepiece to the journey – we will go through the song-suite chronologically. This will help us understand how the journey progresses.

The journey

'The Ninth Wave' begins with 'And Dream of Sheep.' A calm introduction, it sees the BFS struggle to stay conscious as they float upon water. The story behind this part of the song-suite is described as follows:

> It's the idea of this person being in the water, how they've got there, we don't know. But the idea is that they've been on a ship and they've been washed over the side so they're alone in this water... And they've got a life jacket with a little light so that if anyone should be travelling at night they'll see the light and know they're there... the idea that they've got it in their head that they mustn't fall asleep, because if you fall asleep when you're in the water, I've heard that you roll over and so you drown, so they're trying to keep themselves awake.[8]

While the song presents the literal struggle to stay awake, at a more metaphorical level the cycle introduces the struggle between conscious and unconscious realities, waking and sleeping, that the journey negotiates. The spontaneous initiatory shamanic crisis that will have to be overcome is intimated by the deep, portentous piano melody that intrudes upon the song. The BFS sings 'Oh I'll wake up to any sound of engines' (*HL*) before returning to the calmer piano parts.

As the song phase moves on, the music flows into the unconscious dreamscapes of 'Under Ice.' Populated by distant echoing screams and thunder storms, it is also accentuated by layered deep vocals sung over threatening, synthesized cello sounds. In the landscape of the song the BFS skates, making lines over a river that has frozen over, skimming over the ice and past trees 'splitting' and 'spitting' 'sound' (*HL*). The mental distress that is essential to the challenge of the rebirth journey or 'shamanic illness' begins to creep in. The music communicates that there is a life trapped under the ice on which the BFS, in her dreams, is skating: 'There's something moving under/ Under the ice,/ Moving under ice – through the water' (*HL*). While we learn that '"It's me"/ Something, someone – help them' (*HL*).

After the final '"It's me"' the vocal falls away. This compounds the sense of being trapped within the journey. The suite moves into a piano-led linking sequence that creates a sense of drowsy unreality, blurring the distinction between conscious and unconscious states. This places the listener in an altered state essential to the undertaking of a shamanic journey. A number of different voices coax the BFS to wake up - 'You must wake up!' (*HL*), 'Wake up child, pay attention' (*HL*). This conjures a return to childhood as various authoritarian voices (the parent, the schoolteacher) impel the BFS to emerge from sleep.

Being told to 'wake up,' of course, has a number of meanings. It can be connected to gaining enlightenment, as the 'little light' (*HL*) motif which weaves in and out of the soundscape, suggests. It is arguably this very search for enlightenment that the journey attempts through the crisis-dominated shamanic journey. Other voices help search for this knowledge: 'can you not see that little light?' 'Where?' 'Over here' (*HL*). The quest is punctuated by uncertainty as sampled voices tell the speaker to wake up. These are disturbed by crowds of voices which clutter the space, dispelling the sensory equilibrium that had been present until this stage of the journey.

As the voices slowly fall away, a final voice utters: 'Look who's here to see you' (*HL*). This initiates the moment where the music passes into a new threshold of sonic storytelling. It is a space that is fractured, intense and troubling, and comes to symbolise the beginning of the spontaneous shamanic crisis. The BFS's voice splinters and chokes over the top of a rolling synthesizer sequence, punctuated by chaotic drums - 'Listen to me, listen to me, talk to me, help me, talk to me' (*HL*) - as the broken vocals simulate the drowning of the BFS within the soundscape. This vocal effect is repeated later on in the song to convey the sense of desperation and persecution essential to later stages of the journey. This technological fracturing of the voice breaks up language within the song.

The female voice stutters and splinters in the face of the law represented in 'Waking the Witch.' This portrays the interaction between an accused woman and the law persecuting her for her perceived wrongdoing. The use of voice in this way *allows* the BFS to represent how the female voice is allowed to operate within a male-defined legal judgement that cannot *hear* the female voice speaking.

'Waking the Witch' presents the chaotically splintered female voice and juxtaposes it with the deep and authoritative male voice in a witch trial. Juxtaposing male and female voices in confrontational ways is a familiar tactic of the BFS. We have seen a similar vocal duel in the climax to 'Get out of My House' on *The Dreaming*. In 'Get out of My House' the BFS holds her vocal ground, transforming into a mule as an act of resistance. The interaction between the male and female voice on 'Waking the Witch' however, is clearly an unequal one. Structured by hierarchical relations, this doesn't allow for women to participate equally to men.

This difference in status is communicated by the contrast in tones, as the male voice is hyper-masculine, sounding like a mythical ogre. His voice occupies a fragile border between humour and terror: 'You won't burn/ You won't bleed/ Confess to me girl – Go down' (*HL*). The authoritative voice is counter-posed by the BFS's vocals that mimic nursery rhymes - 'red red roses, pinks and posies' (*HL*) - that recall childhood and invoke protection. The music then switches to the sound of chanting and church bells, further evoking the situation of the witch trial as the congregation casts judgement upon her. The BFS has taken on the role of the witch who has become the main figure in the rebirth journey.

This moment signals a movement into the Underworld. The sequence is then repeated before the BFS's vocals again become fractured, running over the nursery-rhyme lyrics as the climax to the trial occurs. It appears the witch is about to be drowned. She has a stone around her leg, while the stuttering, effected vocals communicate her final act of drowning.

The lyrics of the song offer a description of the unfair trial: 'Bless me father, bless me father for I have sinned.../ I question your innocence' (*HL*). The BFS then evokes a blackbird for protection: '(Help this blackbird, there's a stone round my leg)/ "She's a witch"/ (Help this blackbird, there's a stone round my leg)/ "Uh, Damn you woman!"' (*HL*).

As the BFS sings the line about the blackbird, her vocal departs in high tones, marking off a resistant space. The isolated witch articulates her affinity with the blackbird in a scene where human relationships only yield punishment. The blackbird is the witch's 'familiar' – a spirit ally that could appear in human or animal form. In witch trials authorities used familiars as evidence of 'the direct, and probably sexual, link assumed to exist between the Devil and the accused, and also showing the way both spirits and witchcraft skills were thought to be handed on from woman to woman.'[9] Blackbirds have appeared before as allies to the BFS - we have already explored the BFS's affinity in the 'And So Is Love' video.

The vocal line which connects the blackbird and the witch creates a point of survival. This enables endurance outside the boundaries of the trial that, with a barrage of male and female voices, condemn her as '(Guilty, Guilty, Guilty)' (*HL*). The pain and terror of this scene is furthered by the BFS's groans that choke between the terrifying crowds of noise.

After 'Waking the Witch,' the journey moves into a post-traumatic space of 'Watching You Without Me.' We are told to 'Get out of the Waves, Get out of the water' (*HL*) as the music seems to move into the arena of absence, or death. Moving into this song transforms the time frame from the witch trials into a more modern setting. This again affirms the shift between conscious and unconscious realities, or the shamanistic ability to move between the two states of life and death.

Entering into the space of death or absence is essential to the rebirth journey: it is an experience of living death, which has to occur if one is to be reborn - death must occur at a deeply psychic level. This revisits a similar theme from 'All the Love' on *The Dreaming* which articulates the perspective of death within life. In that song friends gather round the 'dead' speaker trying to communicate and be let into the world characterised by her departure.

In 'Watching You Without Me' the BFS on her journey seems to be dead. She watches a lover or friend walk around the house as they wait fruitlessly for her to arrive. She attempts to communicate but is not able to be heard: 'You can't hear me/ You can't hear me/ You can't hear what I'm saying/ You can't hear what I'm saying to you' (*HL*).

The radical absence is highlighted in the lines 'I'm not here, but I'm not here, but I'm not here' (*HL*). The BFS is a voyeuristic ghost. The song offers a space of grief and mourning, but reverses the usual position of the living mourning the dead. Instead the dead articulate their frustration in not being able to communicate with the living, which opens up awareness of a world that co-exists with the living one. As in the Emily Dickinson poem, 'This World is not Conclusion./ A Species stands beyond—.'[10]

The traumatic splintering of voice and language – which has now come to operate as a traumatic motif – is worked through again at the end of the song: 'Listen to me, listen to Me, talk to Me' (*HL*). This repeats the shifts of time and memory outside the calm and detached space of death the song provides, into the chaos of the journey and the challenges it presents.

After death there will be birth. The excited violin riff beckons us to join in the 'Jig of Life.' It is here that the witch appears again in the story in a moment of identification that forms the journey's dramatic peak. This time the witch is not demonised by the community wishing to punish her for her 'sins.' She is given an important space to connect with another female character. This creates an intense female homosocial and homoerotic connection. 'Hello old lady/ I know your face well' (*HL*). The face of the witch is familiar and can be read as a reflection of the BFS's stronger self. Confronting her enables movement forward on her journey: 'She says Oh-na-na-na-na-na/ I'll be sitting in your mirror/ Now is the place where the crossroads meet/ Will you look into the future' (*HL*).

The witch offers the BFS a glimpse of self-reflection and identification – a female homoerotic relation that orientates her toward the future. This moment of lesbian identification is critical for securing a place for autonomous female sexuality within male-defined cultures. These have traditionally refused women the place of autonomous desiring subject and the lesbian is the key to accessing that desire.

The encounter dramatised in 'The Jig of Life' represents what Teresa de Lauretis describes as lesbianism as 'an envisaged possibility... [that] can serve to guarantee "women" the status of sexed and desiring subjects, wherever their desire may be directed in psychosocial reality.'[11] That is, one does not need to sleep with women to benefit from the power of lesbian desire. The importance of lesbianism for securing an active and independent desire for women, she argues, needs to be acknowledged.

As the confrontation continues, the 'woken' spirit, desire and energy of the witch is integrated. She demands her to: 'Never, never say goodbye/ To my part of your life,' while impelling the BFS to 'let me live/ She said c'mon let me live/ She said c'mon let me live girl' (*HL*).

The lyrics and music demand the retrieval of independent female desire. They celebrate that desire as dynamic and embedded within living culture. Both lyrics and music communicate this through their insistence, leading to exuberant expression. The force of the witch's story is essential to empowering the BFS on her rebirth journey. It operates potently, conjoining female-identification and desire.

The present moment is a reclamation of the past: 'This moment in time/ It doesn't belong to you,/ It belongs to me' (*HL*). The ancient force of the encounter is further suggested by the lines 'Where on your palm is my little line/ When you're written in mine,/ As an old memory' (*HL*). This suggests the continuing lineage of these energies and their abilities to endure across space and time. They direct the destiny of the shamanic heroine on the journey's path.

The importance of memory is what drives the search for submerged histories as they are scattered about the body of the song: 'I put this moment here' (*HL*). This phrase is repeated, the scattered effect communicated by being placed in different positions within the mix. Listeners are embroiled in the search for memories at a physical, sonic level.

The spoken-word poem narrated by John Carder Bush also contains a reference to past lives, 'Time in her eyes is spawning past life,/ One with the ocean and the woman unfurled'[12] (*HL*), that further underlines how the song functions to unearth and recall past lives and histories. The female-centred relationship that the song explicitly celebrates is crucial for the movement forward in the journey – the importance of retrieving memory and embedding it within the dynamic consciousness of life.

As the final chord struck from 'Jig of Life' resonates, the music is transported back again to a more modern time setting. This is communicated by the technologically-mediated voice asking 'where were you at nine times the speed of sound?' (*HL*) This statement creates a fast dimensional shift between worlds, inaugurating a new sphere of reality. After the crisis and process of initiation, here is an altogether different space. It is characterised by a solid sense of equilibrium evoked by the startled, but self-present clarity of 'Hello Earth.'

The song offers a space of recuperation as the BFS tentatively glimpses stability: 'Peek-a-boo,/ Peek-a-boo, Little Earth' (*HL*). The invocation to the earth suggests balance and grounding. This is reflected in the music that veers between 1980s emotional power ballad and otherwordly gothic chorus, inspired by the score for the 1922 vampire film *Nosferatu*.

The song repeats the phrase 'Get out of the Waves, get out of the water' used earlier in the song-suite, as water and waves symbolise danger, change and transformation, which is contrasted with the solidity of the earth's poise. This sequence becomes the dramatic, elevated chorus used to declare a homecoming for estranged sailors. The song becomes a soothing lullaby for the earth, 'Go to Sleep Little Earth' (*HL*).

It is in this part of the journey that the language of birth and rebirth becomes most explicit: 'I was there at the birth,/ Out of the cloud burst the head of the Tempest,/ Murderer, Murderer, of calm' (*HL*). Here the BFS bears witness to her experience during the journey, the destruction or murder of calm that the journey created, whilst articulating ambivalence and confusion as to why she was chosen to undertake it: '*Why did I go?*' (*HL*, italics mine). After this sequence ends with the rising vocal that falls into the vampire chorus, a new passage in the journey of transformation is marked. Here the music draws into a misty soundscape that appears to offer no clarity or exit. That is until the full stages of enlightenment and integration of the journey's lessons that 'The Morning Fog' celebrates.

Grof argues that 'to be recognized as a shaman requires successful completion of the initiatory crisis, integration of the achieved insights, and attainment of adequate or superior functioning in everyday reality.'[13] Returning to the everyday reality of family relationships and valuing them with renewed vigour, is precisely what occurs on 'The Morning Fog.' The enlightenment is itself physical, splitting, vocal: 'The light/ Begin to Bleed,/ Begin to breath/ Begin to speak' (*HL*).

The image here of intense, porous luminosity engulfs the BFS in moments of contentment. The lesson gained on the rebirth journey is to learn how to love better and appreciate the family relationships around her: 'I'll kiss the ground,/ I'll tell my mother/...How much I love them' (*HL*) and 'D'you know what?/ I love you better now' (*HL*). The spectrum of family ties the song celebrates – Mother, Father, Brothers - suggest the importance and strength of these bonds. The process of rebirth is free-falling and transcendent, uplifted by the fretless bass and constant light drum machine sequence. The ascendant guitar riffs evoke pleasant strains of joy, relief and peace. Rebirth is again articulated in the second verse as the liberated fall toward death demonstrates the proximate position to life and death the shaman harbours: 'I am falling/ Like a stone,/ Like a storm/ Being born again' (*HL*).

After the manifold struggles of the rebirth journey – its adventures through submerged mythical Underworlds and its intimate courting of death – the sequence ends with the positive strains of 'The Morning Fog.' The song conveys the feeling of survival and completion of a journey that ends with return.

The whole of 'The Ninth Wave' offers a dramatic exploration of the theme of rebirth. Rebirth is essential to the BFS's capacity to generate new forms of subjectivity which has been consistent throughout her life. It is an important theme in the literal return of the BFS on 2005's *Aerial*. This is the final part of our journey with the BFS. *Aerial* is the moment of her final disappearance. It presents her escape from subjectivity itself.

Aerial: the return and disappearance of the BFS

Employing a similar structure to the *Hounds of Love*, *Aerial* is split into two sections – one a collection of songs, the other an extended song-suite, 'A Sky of Honey,' which I will be focussing on. To understand how the BFS can return on *Aerial*, we need to consider how she (re)created space for herself after her enclosure and suicide on T*he Red Shoes*. We need to understand how space is opened up on the work. The BFS needed a conceptual shift so she could return. She needed to invent new rules that would allow her to live.

Aerial marks a turning point in the history of the BFS's cover art. She had slowly been disappearing from her album covers. *Aerial* is the moment of disappearance, and presents a picture of a sound wave, doubling up as an image of rocks and their shadowy reflection against the sea. This creates space that is refreshingly expansive. The title of the album itself conjures freedom, both within space, and to see things from the air.

The first part of the album charts an intimate and familiar interiority in the BFS's music. There are songs about domestic alienation ('Mrs. Bartolozzi'), mother-son relationships ('Bertie'), and bereavement ('A Coral Room'). In some senses this collection of songs is the BFS's most intimate ever. They delve deeply into personal observances, and can be seen as the inverse of the other part of the album.

The second song-suite, while following a similar pattern to 'The Ninth Wave,' opens up new sonic and spatial territories. This opening up of space is not merely coincidental. It emerges from a displacement of an anthropocentric, humanist focus. This kind of strategy, you will remember, was present earlier in the BFS's life, most notably on *The Dreaming*. It can be seen as an important tactic in her work. Displacing anthropocentrism enables the BFS to explore other relationships and connections with non-human actors, namely the 'languages' of light, animals and birdsong. The 'Prelude' states: 'The day is full of birds/ Sounds like they're saying words.'[14]

'A Sky of Honey' can also be read as a rebirth narrative. It charts the cycle of day to night, and is similarly concerned with the processes of emergence and renewal that dominate 'The Ninth Wave.' However, what marks the difference between the two works is a greater engagement with the cycles and rhythms of the *natural* world, rather than the anthropocentric cosmologies which underpin 'The Ninth Wave.' This is the conceptual move that creates much-needed space for the BFS. It enables new configurations, connections and possibilities to occur.

Within traditional humanist discourses, animals are not thought to have the same access to language as humans. Often animal language is dismissed by human culture because it is not seen as intellectually viable. Descartes stated:

> It is not the want of organs that brings this to pass, for it is evident that magpies and parrots are able to utter words

> just like ourselves, and yet they cannot speak as we do, that is, so as to give evidence *that they think of what they say.*[15]

However in 'A Sky of Honey' the language of animals, and specifically birdsong, is taken seriously. It refuses to see human language as superior to animals. It is this conceptual shift towards listening and the desire to listen to animal language that opens up space for the BFS to (re)emerge. It enables new possible spheres of understanding within the song-suite. It helps move listeners' attention away from the exclusive perception of human beings, allowing for a consideration of nonhuman life: the particles of light and melodies of bird song.

'A Sky of Honey' also signals the final transformation of the BFS. She merges with her environment. As she engages with non-human life she is not subject to a framework of being structured by divisions. These divisions (subject/object) separate humans from the world, often enforcing an idea that they are superior to other forms of life (animals, the earth as a whole). An alternative orientation is presented in 'A Sky of Honey.' As we move away from perceptions dominated by human interests, the possibility of mutual patterns of inter-relation with the non or unhuman life forces can emerge. The BFS 'becomes imperceptible':

> Becoming-imperceptible is the point of fusion between the self and his or her habitat, the cosmos as a whole. It marks the point of evanescence of the self and its replacement by a living nexus of interconnections that empower not the self, but the collective, not identity, but affirmative subjectivity, not consciousness, but affirmative interconnections.[16]

Within 'A Sky of Honey' the human is one life force among many that populate the earth. None is seen to eclipse the other: instead, they are mutually interconnected. In its universe we are made conscious of the ever-changing patterns of light - 'all the time, the light is changing' (*A*) - as this motif is repeated through the suite. The light becomes connected with the changing colour of the painting which also forms part of the narrative of the cycle. The painting is also exposed to the natural elements that transform its intended meaning as time, light and substance shift - 'all the colours run' (*A*). This is reminiscent of the bleeding light in 'The Morning Fog.'

We are reintroduced to familiar birds that have populated the BFS's life. The 'blackbirds sing at dusk' (*A*), revive the memory of the birds' connection with the witch on *Hounds of Love*, and its link with death in the video for 'And So Is Love.' The BFS has created her own mythological universe in her life. Symbols are reclaimed from enclosure on *The Red Shoes*, as the blackbirds inaugurate the sunset, singing life into the cycle of the day.

It is in the final song of the suite, 'Aerial,' that the climax of communication with bird-song occurs: 'Oh the dawn has come/ And the song must be sung/ And the flowers are melting/ What kind of language is this?' (*A*).

'What kind of language is this?' recognises bird-song as language. It sees it as valid communication with its own possibility of meaning. Importantly the BFS does not suggest we can *understand* this language: 'I can't hear a word you're saying/ Tell me what you are singing' (*A*). This is crucial because it establishes the positive difference of the bird-song. It states proximity, but not a reduction to sameness. This is the space of becoming that we explored on *The Dreaming*. The final song of the suite institutes a space of becoming birdsong. We have travelled through the night-and-day to move finally at sunset into the physical space of birdsong: 'I feel I want to be up on the roof/ I feel I gotta get up on the roof/ Up, up on the roof' (*A*).

The BFS also demonstrates the *similarity* between animal language and other forms of human communication which are not linguistically based, such as laughter. Here she suggests that aspects of human communication are close to certain forms of animal communication. This presents a potential space of kinship between bird language and human language: 'All of the birds are laughing/ Come on let's all join in' (*A*).

The use of laughter is crucial to the build-up of the song. In the breaks between songs bird-song is placed beside maniacal laughter suggesting, through proximity, the kinship between these two forms of communication. This lends the song an ambience of hysteria, accentuated by the repetitive pulsating drum beat that evokes the rhythms of 1990s rave music. The climax to the song comprises of a euphoric guitar riff, as the BFS's vocals are distorted and filtered, confusing their coherence in the body of the song that revels in the ascendant finale.

As this process builds, further layers of laughter are placed on top of the rising chaos. This lends these 'othered' or non-linguistic forms of human communication an important position in the closing moments of the song, and the album as a whole. As the laughter ends, the final 'word' is, however, given to the birdsong. This exudes the space of the song and ultimately endures the process of the song cycle, symbolising eternity and life-cycles of music independent of human creations.

A further instance of kinship is pointed to within the album's artwork. The three images of the clothes drying on a washing line transform in the third image to what looks like bird's wings flapping. This again marks a space of proximity between the lives and patterns of human beings and birds. It suggests the fluidity of bodies and positions, even in the most domestic of circumstances.

This shift towards recognising a different species of voice is a conceptual shift that creates new conceptions of space within the BFS's life. Moving away from a strictly anthropocentric focus enables new connections and relationships to manifest. It is why the *possibility* of return is realised at the level of physical and sonic space on the record. As well as becoming familiar with these different voices, we return with a sense of the possibility of flight and the perspective of birds: a viewpoint which is necessarily 'of the air.'

With the return to the motif of flight, and the spatial dynamics, the limitations of human culture do not have the same power to contain imaginative leaps. This is not to say that there are *no* limitations, because humans, and perhaps all creatures, will always be limited by how much their body and emotions can take. Importantly, humanist ideas are displaced. Through this displacement whole new worlds of possibilities and interconnections emerge.

This further connects the BFS with shamanic practices, as shamans 'work not so much by contacting supernatural forces as by working with the powers and awareness of the insects, birds, animals, and other nonhuman beings around us.'[17] This time her shamanism is grounded within those relationships of the living, breathing world.

The rebirth journey in 'A Sky of Honey'

'A Sky of Honey' contains a rebirth journey that has similarities as well as differences to 'The Ninth Wave.' As a journey it is primarily concerned with mapping the cycles of the day in motions of constant renewal: 'Oh so exciting, mmh go on and on/ Every time you leave us/ So Summer will be gone/ So you'll never grow old to us' (*A*).

This passage from the 'Prologue' celebrates infinite and self-renewing cycles, while the slow music gives the impression of a reflective afternoon. Slower and ambient music dominates the first half of the song-suite, as the journey moves through the song of the 'oil and the brush' (*A*). This song engages with a process of painting, highlighting mistakes as an important part of artistic creativity: 'That bit there, it was an accident/ But he's so pleased/ It's the best mistake, he could make' (*A*).

It is in this song that listeners are made conscious of the shifting light, 'all the time/ The light is changing' (*A*), that will be so important for the motifs of the suite as it passes through the changing cycles of the day. The lumbering pace picks up at 'Sunset.' It is at night-time when the greatest transformations occur to the fabric of light, as perspectives are subject to radical change. Like a painting, this is explored through colour: 'Whose shadow, long and low/ Is slipping out of wet clothes?' as it 'changes into/ The most beautiful/ Iridescent blue' (*A*).

The importance of light and colour to the song cannot be underestimated. It is through it the language of transformation and decay is communicated: 'This is a song of colour/ Where sands sing in crimson, red and rust/ Then climb into bed and turn to dust' (*A*).

This part of the suite relates how the natural cycles of the day create space for different perspectives and possibilities to emerge. The fact that it is at night-time when the greatest transformations occur creates continuity with the journey into the Underworld that is explored on 'The Ninth Wave.' The liminal spaces of 'Somewhere Inbetween' (day/ night, life/ death) evoke the spirit of the shamanistic journey that shifts and moves between spaces and states, while in 'Nocturn,' 'We dive deeper and deeper' (*A*).

'Nocturn' in particular seems to point towards a desire to revisit the Underworld as 'We long for just that something more' (*A*). This song blurs the distinction between conscious and unconscious realities as the BFS deploys dreamlike scenarios - 'We stand in the Atlantic' (*A*) - to accentuate the altered state depicted in the song, as 'We swim further and further/ We dive down' (*A*).

The importance of space to this journey should be recalled now, as it is here that 'we become panoramic' (*A*). This offers an exultant description of spatial liberation essential for opening up the creativity of the song-suite. In the closing moments of 'Nocturn,' we glimpse the ascendance of the sun as the piece moves toward the melodramatic climax. The motifs of light and movement coalesce, as the familiar use of male chorus voices in the BFS's music heralds the sun rising in the sky: 'Look at the light, all the time it's a changing' as it becomes 'bright, white coming alive jumping off of the aerial/ All the time it's a changing, like now.../ All the time it's a changing, like then again...' (*A*).

In the finale to this song, the natural world itself, with its multiplicity of shifting lights, is afforded the shamanistic qualities. These are usually assigned to the hero who undertakes the journey. Here the boundless energetic vitality of the world is offered as a dynamic force that can be productively engaged with in order to explore visionary possibilities. The ascendant transformation that brings light into the day reminds listeners of the constant and daily cycles of renewal and rebirth, the intimate proximity with life and death, and the constancy of shifting between these states.

With the BFS's own musical return on this album, there is a continuation of her concern to explore patterns and journeys that focus on renewal. There is the important move away from the *singular* rebirth of the BFS, as her life becomes embedded within the multiple destinies of all life forces, channelled on this work through the focus on light and birdsong. She finally embraces 'the floodgate of creative forces that make it possible to be actually fully inserted into [...] the present unfolding of potentials.'[18]

These potentials are located in space and flight. They offer 'panoramic' (*A*) proportions and help open up perspectives. They offer new dynamics of space from which future creative endeavours can spring in the mutually affirmative space between human and non human life. The constancy of renewal and cycles ensure that one thing is certain in the life of the BFS. That any departure will be met with the promise of return, and that all that ends will be reborn.

Notes

Adventures in Kate Bush and Theory: Introduction

1. John Lydon, quoted in 'Queens of British Pop,' *BBC One*, April 2009.
2. Bob Mercer, Interviewed on 'Queens of British Pop,' *BBC One*, April 2009. The interview was referring to the sexist marketing policy of EMI, who Kate Bush signed to when she was 16.
3. Mark Radcliffe, 'The Smouldering Gypsy Lover We Would Never Have,' in *The Word*, February 2009, Issue 72, p.95
4. There are a number of different Kate Bush fan communities and forums. These include *The Homeground and Kat Bush News and Information Forum* (http://thehomegroundandkatebushnewsandinfoforum.yuku.com/); *The Kate Bush Forum* (http://www.katebushforum.com/forum/) and *The Sensual World of Kate Bush* (http://katebush.proboards.com/index.cgi). They often provide lively and challenging discussions of Bush's music.
5. See Krystyna Fitzgerald-Morris, Peter Fitzgerald-Morris and David Cross (eds.), *HomeGround: The Kate Bush Magazine* (1982 – present). Available online at: http://www.katebushnews.com/homegrou.htm. Last accessed: 18 Oct 2008.
6. See Holly Kruse, 'In Praise of Kate Bush,' in Simon Frith and Peter Goodwin (eds.), *On Record: Rock, Pop and the Written Word* (London: Routledge, 1990), pp.50–465; Nicky Losseff, 'Cathy's Homecoming and the Other World: Kate Bush's "Wuthering Heights",' *Popular Music* 18 (1999), pp.227-240; Laura Vroomen, *This Woman's Work: Kate Bush Fans and Practices of Distinction* (Unpublished PhD thesis, Warwick, 2003); Bonnie Gordon, 'Kate Bush's Subversive Shoes,' in *Women and Music: A Journal of Gender and Culture* 9 (2005), pp.37-50; Emma Mayhew, 'Positioning the Producer: Gender Divides in Creative Labour and Value,' in Andrew Bennett, Stan Hawkins and Sheila Whiteley (eds.), *Music, Space and Place: Popular Music and Cultural Identity* (Aldershot: Ashgate, 2004), pp.147-154; Sheila Whiteley, 'Kate Bush: The Red Shoes,' in *Too Much, Too Young: Popular Music, Age and Gender* (London: Routledge, 2005), pp.70-84 and Ron Moy, *Kate Bush and Hounds of Love* (Aldershot: Ashgate, 2007).

7 You will find an inspiring introduction to the concept of subjectivity with Lisa Blackman et al., 'Creating Subjectivities' in *Subjectivity* (2008) 22, 1-27.

8 See Vroomen for interesting perspectives about how Kate Bush's (mainly female) fans use her music to negotiate their lives and identities.

9 *Ibid*, p.16.

10 Judith Butler, *Frames of War: When is Life Grievable?* (London: Verso, 2009), p.52.

11 Cavarero, Adriana, *For More Than One Voice: Towards a Philosophy of Vocal Expression* (Stanford: Stanford University Press, 2005), p.12.

12 See Luce Irigaray, *This Sex Which is Not One*, trans. Catherine Porter (Ithaca: Cornell University Press, 1985).

13 Cavarero, p.8.

14 Susan McClary, *Feminine Endings*, (Minnesota: University of Minnesota Press, 1991), p.136. Italics mine.

15 I am spelling 'magickal' in this way, instead of 'magical,' to make explicit the link between Bush's strategies and the occult.

The Kick Inside: The Beginning of the Journey

1 Xavière Gauthier, 'Why Witches?' in Elaine Marks and Isabelle de Courtivron (eds.), *New French Feminisms: An Anthology* (New York: Harvester, 1981), pp.199-203 (p.199). First italics in original, second italics in mine.

2 *Ibid.*

3 *Ibid.*

4 Cavarero, p.5.

5 *Ibid.*

6 Losseff, p.229.

7 As quoted in Harry Doherty, 'The Kick Outside,' *Melody Maker* (3 June 1978).

8 As quoted in David Wigg, 'Wuthering Wonderful,' *Daily Express* (8 Mar 1978).

9 See Dale Spender, *Man-Made Language* (London: Pandora, 1980), p.39 for a discussion about this.

10 Dickinson, '1383,' in Thomas H. Johnson (ed.), *Emily Dickinson: The Complete Poems* (London: Faber, 1975), p.594.

11 Kate Bush, *The Kick Inside* (EMI: EMC 3223 OC 062 06 603), 1978. Italics mine. All other references to the album will appear abbreviated in parentheses after the quotation (*KT*).

12 Luce Irigaray, 'Introduction: Spirituality and Religion,' in Luce Irigaray (ed.), *Key Writings* (London: Continuum, 2004), pp.145-150 (p.146).

13 Luce Irigaray, 'How Can We Live Together in a Lasting Way?' in Luce Irigaray (ed.), *Key Writings* (London: Continuum, 2004) pp.123-133 (p.127).

14 Luce Irigaray, 'When our lips speak together,' in Janet Price and Margrit Shildrick (eds.), *Feminist Theory and the Body: A Reader* (Edinburgh: Edinburgh University Press, 1999), pp.82-91 (p. 88).

15 Keith Negus, 'Sinead O'Connor – Musical Mother,' in Sheila Whiteley (ed.), *Sexing the Groove: Popular Music and Gender* (London: Routledge, 1997), pp.180–195 (p.180).

16 Irigaray, 'Our Lips,' p.85.

17 Irigaray quoted in Sheila Whiteley, *Popular Music and Feminine Sexuality, Identity and Subjectivity* (London, Routledge, 2000), p.120.

18 Elizabeth Grosz, *Volatile Bodies* (Bloomington: Indiana University Press), p.7.

19 Brandon Labelle, *Background Noise: A History of Sound Art* (London: Continuum, 2006), p.xi.

20 Elizabeth Grosz, *Volatile Bodies* (Bloomington: Indiana University Press), p.5.

21 Elizabeth Wood, 'Sapphonics', in Philip Brett, Elizabeth Wood and Gary C. Thomas (eds.), *Queering the Pitch: The New Gay and Lesbian Musicology* (London: Routledge, 1994), pp.27-66 (p.28).

22 *Ibid*, p.33.

23 Peter Reilly, 'Uncaged Bird,' review of *The Kick Inside*, *Stereo* (1978).

24 Irigaray quoted in Sheila Whiteley, *Feminine*, p.121. Italics mine.

25 Adrienne Rich (1981) *Compulsory Heterosexuality and Lesbian Existence* (London: Only Women Press).

26 See, for example, Carol P. Christ and Judith Plaskow (eds.), *Womanspirit Rising: A Feminist Reader in Religion* (San Francisco: Harper Collins, 1992). First published in 1979, it is a good collection detailing the various positions relating to feminist spirituality.

27 Carol P. Christ, *Rebirth of the Goddess: Finding Meaning in Feminist Spirituality* (London: Routledge, 2004), p.xiii.

28 *Ibid*, p.89.

29 *Ibid.*

30 Luce Irigaray, *Sexes and Genealogies*, trans. Gillian C. Gill (New York: Columbia University Press, 1982), p.64.

31 Marie Mulvey Roberts, 'Menstrual Misogyny and Taboo: The Medusa, Vampire and Female Stigmatic,' in Andrew Shail and Gillian Howie (eds.), *Menstruation: A Cultural History* (Basingstoke: Palgrave, 2005), pp.149-161 (p.149).

32 Penelope Shuttle and Peter Redgrove, *The Wise Wound: Menstruation and Everywoman* (London: Paladin, 1986), p.363.

33 Ernst Lehner and Johanna Lehner, *Folklore and Symbolism of Flowers, Plants and Trees* (London: Dover Publications, 2004), p.54.

34 Shuttle and Redgrove, p.262.

35 *Ibid*, p.197.

36 Gauthier, p.199.

37 Cixous, Hélène, 'The Laugh of the Medusa,' in Robyn R. Warhol and Diane Price Herndl (eds.), *Feminisms: An Anthology of Literary Theory and Criticism* (Basingstoke: Macmillan, 1997), pp.335-342, (p.337).

38 *Ibid*, p.337.

39 The Au Pairs, *Sense and Sensuality*, B00005V330, 1982, 2002.

40 Reilly. Italics mine.

41 Michelle Boulous Walker, *Philosophy and the Maternal Body: Reading Silence* (London: Routledge, 1999), p.135.

42 Kate Bush, 'Self Portrait,' *The Kick Inside* promo LP/cassette interview (1978).

43 Anon, 'The Story of Lucy Wan,' in A.L Lloyd and R. Vaughan Williams (eds.), The Penguin Book of English Folk Songs (London: Penguin, 1961), p.65.

44 *Ibid.*

45 *Ibid.*

46 *Ibid.*

47 *Ibid.*

Lionheart and the Queer Life of the BFS

1 X-Ray Spex, *The Anthology* (Castle: CMDDD369 LC 6448), 2001.

2 Ron Jovanovich, *Kate Bush: The Biography* (London: Portrait, 2006), p. 85.

3 I mean this as a joke – the real reason why men played women characters was because woman weren't allowed to perform on stage. This just underlines how restrictive society has been for women.

4 You can watch the performance online here: http://www.youtube.com/watch?v=mYTmGchjG4k last accessed 20 July 2009.

5 *Ibid.*

6 Judith Butler, *Gender Trouble: Feminism and the Subversion of Identity* (London: Routledge, 1993), p.175.

7 *Ibid*, p.178.

8 *Ibid*, p.175.

9 Wood, p.32.

10 *Ibid.*

11 JM Barrie, *Peter Pan in Kensington Gardens/ Peter and Wendy* (Oxford: Oxford World's Classics, 1999).

12 Judith Halberstam, *In a Queer Time and Place: Transgender Bodies, Subcultural Lives* (New York: New York University Press, 2005), p.179.

13 Judith Halberstam, *Female Masculinity* (Durham: Duke University Press, 1998), p.1.

14 Nathan Evans quoted in Erica Jones, 'How Kate Bush has inspired a Gay Cult,' *The Pink Paper* (Sep 2005), pp.26-27 (p.26).

15 Gillian Rodger 'Drag, Camp and Gender Subversion in the music and video of Annie Lennox,' *Popular Music* 23: 1 (2004), pp.17-29 (p.26).

16 Richard Dyer, *The Culture of Queers* (London: Routledge, 2002), p.60. Italics mine.

17 Rodger, p.26.

18 Christopher Isherwood, as quoted in Dyer, p.26

19 As quoted in Kate Bush, 'Hello Everybody,' *KBC* 2 (Summer 1979). Available online: http://gaffa.org/garden/kate2.html. Last accessed : 13 Oct 2008.

20 As quoted in Anon, '*Lionheart* Promo Cassette,' EMI Canada (1978). Available online: http://gaffa.org/reaching/im78_lh.html. Last accessed: 13 Oct 2008.

21 Moy, p.22.

22 Kate Bush, 'Kate's KBC article,' *KBC* 3 (Nov 1979). Available online: http://gaffa.org/garden/kate3.html. Last accessed: 13 October 2008.

23 As quoted in Doherty, 'Kick.'

24 Roger Sabin, '"I won't let that dago by": Rethinking Punk and Racism,' in Roger Sabin (ed.), *Punk Rock, So What?: The Cultural Legacy of Punk* (London: Routledge, 1999), pp.199–219 (p.199).

25 *Ibid*, p.200.

26 Terry Slater, quoted in Fred Vermorel, *Secret History of Kate Bush: And the Strange Art of Pop* (London: Omnibus Press, 1983), p.92.

27 Ron Moy, 'A Daughter of Albion? Kate Bush and mythologies of Englishness,' *Popular Musicology Online* (2006). Available online: http://www.popular-musicology-online.com/issues/02/moy-01.html. Last accessed: 15 Oct 2007.

28 Vermorel, p.35.

29 Vroomen, p.265.

30 *Ibid*, p.267.

31 *Ibid.*

32 As quoted in Anon, '*Lionheart* Promo.' Italics mine.

33 Whiteley, *Too Much*, p.73.

34 Vroomen, p.267.

35 As quoted in Ed Stewart and Sue Cook, 'Personal Call,' *BBC Radio 1* interview (1979). Available online: http://gaffa.org/reaching/ir79_pc.html. Last accessed 13 Oct 2008.

36 Hugh Charles and Ross Parker, 'There'll always be an England,' *Sterling Times: The Virtual Scrapbook of British Nostalgia*. Available online http://www.sterlingtimes.co.uk/alwaysengland.html. Last accessed: 13 Oct 2008.

37 Ibid.

38 See A.L. Macfie, 'Introduction', in A.L. Macfie (ed.), *Orientalism: A Reader* (Edinburgh: Edinburgh University Press, 2000), pp.2-17 (p. 3). The field was also shaped by Homi Bhabha, *The Location of Culture* (London: Routledge, 1994) who critiqued the Western tendency to represent non-Western cultures in terms of binary oppositions and Gayatri Chakravorty Spivak, 'Can the Subaltern Speak?' in Cary Nelson and Larry Grossberg (eds.), *Marxism and the Interpretation of Culture* (Urbana, Illinois: University of Illinois Press, 1988),

pp.271-313, which questioned the idea of whether subaltern subjects, such as the Third World woman, could ever 'speak' within the terms defined by Western, imperialist discourse.

39 Macfie, 'Introduction,' p.6.

40 Simon Schaar, 'Orientalism at the Service of Imperialism', in A.L. Macfie (ed.), *Orientalism: A Reader* pp.181-193 (p.182).

41 Derek B. Scott, *From the Erotic to the Demonic* (Oxford: Oxford University Press, 2003), p.173.

42 As quoted in Anon, 'KB On Tour,' *Nationwide* TV Programme (4 Apr 1979). Available online: http://gaffa.org/reaching/iv79_ot.html, Last accessed: 13 Oct 2008.

43 Scott, p.161.

44 Joseph Boone, 'Vacation Cruises; or, The Homoerotics of Orientalism,' in John Hawley (ed.), *Post-Colonial, Queer* (New York: SUNY, 2001), pp.43-78 (p.44).

45 Leo Bersani, *Homos* (Cambridge: Harvard University Press, 1995), p.34. Walt Whitman's 'Calamus' poems also link homosexuality, or 'comradeship' as he calls it, with death.

Never for Ever: the continuity and change of the BFS

1 Kate Bush, *Never For Ever* (EMI: 1A 062 07339), 1980. All quotes will hereafter be referred to in capitalized initials in parentheses after quote (*NFE*).

2 Boone, p.51.

3 Allyson Mitchell, 'Deep Lez I Statement,' available online http://www.allysonmitchell.com/action/deeplez.cfm. Last accessed 30 Nov 09.

4 Sasha Roseneil, *Disarming Patriarchy: Feminism and Political Action at Greenham* (Buckingham: Open University Press, 1995), p.25.

5 Luce Irigaray, 'The Age of the Breath,' in Luce Irigaray (ed.), *Key Writings* (London: Continuum, 2004), pp.165-170 (p.165).

The Dreaming, the Breakdown and Becomings of the BFS

1 Karen Barad, *Meeting the Universe Halfway: Quantum Physics and the Entanglement of Matter and Meaning* (Durham: Duke University Press, 2007), p.33. Italics in original.

2 Gilles Deleuze and Felix Guattari, *A Thousand Plateaus*, trans. Brian Massumi (London: Continuum, 2004), p.364.

3 Simon Reynolds, *Rip It Up and Start Again: Post Punk 1978-1984* (London: Faber 2005), p.xix.

4 Kate Bush, *The Dreaming* (EMI: EMC 3419 OC 062 64 589), 1982. References to this album will be followed by an italicised *TD* in parentheses after the quote (*TD*).

5 As quoted in Richard Cook, 'My music sophisticated? I'd rather you said that than turdlike!' *New Musical Express* (Oct 1982). Available online: http://gaffa.org/cloud/music/leave_it_open.html. Last accessed: 13 Oct 2008.

6 Deleuze and Guattari, p.300.

7 Haraway, Donna, *Simians, Cyborgs and Women: The Reinvention of Nature* (London: Free Association Books,1991), p.176

8 Donna Haraway, *Modest_Witness@Second Millennium. Female-Man-Meets-Oncomouse: Feminism and Technoscience* (London: Routledge, 1997), p.3.

9 *Ibid*, p. 3.

10 Kate Bush, 'Kate Bush's KBC article' *KBC* 16 (n.d) Available online: http://gaffa.org/garden/kate18.html. Last accessed: 13 Oct 2008.

11 Lynne Hume, 'The Dreaming in Contemporary Aboriginal Australia,' in Graham Harvey (ed.), *Indigenous Religions: A Companion* (London: Cassell, 2000), pp. 124–136, (p.126).

12 Irigaray, 'Spirituality,' p.146.

13 *Ibid*, p.127.

14 As quoted in Anon, 'Unknown BBC interview,' *BBC* (1982). Available online: http://gaffa.org/cloud/music/the_dreaming.html. Last accessed: 13 Oct 2008.

15 Deleuze and Guattari, p.336.

16 Kate Bush, 'Kate's KBC article,' *KBC* 12 (Oct 1982). Available online: http://gaffa.org/garden/kate14.html. Last accessed: 14 Oct 2008.

17 Deleuze and Guattari, p.323.

18 Rosi Braidotti, *Transpositions* (Cambridge: Polity), p. 68.

19 J.C. Cooper, *Symbolic and Mythological Animals* (London: Harper Collins, 1992), p.219

20 Deleuze and Guattari, p.262.

21 *Ibid*, p.262.

22 Braidotti, *Transpositions* (Cambridge: Polity), p.170.

23 Hélène Cixous, 'Sorties Out and Out: Attacks/Ways Out/ Forays' in Hélène Cixous and Catherine Clemènt, *The Newly Born Woman*, trans. Betsy Wing (Manchester: Manchester University Press, 1993), pp.63-134 (p.68).

24 Gayle Rubin, 'The Traffic in Women,' in Linda Nicholson (ed.), *Second Wave Feminism: A Reader* (London: Routledge, 1997), pp.28-67 (p.28).

25 See Elaine Showalter, *The Female Malady: Women, Madness and English Culture, 1830-1980* (London: Virago, 1987), p.11, for an exploration of cultural ideas about proper feminine behaviour, which have shaped the definition and treatment of madness in women in England from 1830-1980, consequently impacting upon their ability to contribute to 'public life.'

26 Ann Cvetkovich, *Archives of Feelings: Trauma and Lesbian Public Cultures* (Durham: Duke University Press, 2003), p. 18.

27 Butler, *Frames*, p.2.

The Red Shoes and the death of the BFS

1 Angela Carter (ed.), *The Virago Book of Fairy Tales* (London: Virago, 1991), p.xxii.

2 See Charlotte Brontë, *Jane Eyre* (London: Penguin, 2006) and Christina Rossetti, 'The Goblin Market' in Christina Rossetti, *The Complete Poems* (London: Penguin, 2001), pp.5-20.

3 Maria Tatar, *Off With Their Heads: Fairy Tales and the Culture of Childhood* (Princeton: Princeton University Press, 1992), p.30.

4 Hans Christian Andersen, 'The Red Shoes,' in *The Complete Fairy Tales* (Ware: Wordsworth, 1998), pp.322-329 (p.328).

5 Bruno Bettleheim, *The Uses of Enchantment: The Meaning and Importance of Fairy Tales* (London: Penguin, 1991), p.8.

6 Hans Christian Andersen, 'The Red Shoes,' in *The Complete Fairy Tales* (Ware: Wordsworth, 1998), pp.322

7 *Ibid*, p.328.

8 *Ibid*, p.325.

9 *Ibid*, p.326.

10 *Ibid.*

11 *Ibid.*

12 *Ibid*, p.328-329.

13 *Ibid*, p.329.

14 Michael Powell and Emeric Pressburger's production name.

15 Ian Christie as quoted in Karli Lukas, 'Dancing with the Devil You Know: On Powell and Pressburger's *The Red Shoes*,' *Senses of Cinema* (July 2005). Available online: http://www.sensesofcinema.com/contents/cteq/05/36/red_shoes.html. Last accessed: 13 Oct 2006.

16 Michael Powell and Emeric Pressburger, *The Red Shoes* (Carlton: VFB22329), 1948, 2001.

17 See Kate Chopin, *The Awakening and Selected Stories*, (London: Penguin, 2003). Edna Pontellier, the main character in *The Awakening* escapes her enclosure within a male defined story through killing herself at the end of the novel.

18 Kate Bush *The Red Shoes* (EMI: B000024BBU),1993. References to the album will be followed by italicized initials in parentheses after quote (*RS*).

19 Bettleheim, p.12.

20 *Ibid*, p.25.

21 Roger Copeland, 'Dance, Feminism and the Critique of the Visual,' in Helen Thomas (ed.), *Dance, Gender and Culture* (Basingstoke: Macmillan, 1993), pp.134–145 (pp. 141). Italics mine.

22 All those girls who wore red shoes,/ Each boarded a train that would not stop./ They could not listen./ They could not stop./ What they did was the death dance./ What they did would do them in. Anne Sexton, 'The Red Shoes,' in Anne Sexton, *Selected Poems of Anne Sexton* (London: Virago, 1993), p.87. You can also see the importance of Powell and Pressburger's film in the line 'each boarded a train that would not stop.'

23 Gordon, p.42.

24 *Ibid*, p.43.

25 Campbell's importance is underlined how he is included on the 'thank you' list in the credits for *The Red Shoes*.

26 Rosemary Ellen Guiley, 'Witchcraft as Goddess Worship,' in Carolyne Addington (ed.), *The Feminist Companion to Mythology* (London: Pandora, 1992), pp.418-425 (p.422).

27 Joseph Campbell, *Hero With a Thousand Faces* (Princeton: Princeton University Press, 1968), p.98.

28 Kate Bush, *The Line, The Cross and the Curve* (PMI: MVN 4911853), 1993. Italics mine.

29 Kate Bush, *Hounds of Love* (EMI: EJ 24 03841), 1985. Subsequent references to the album will appear in parentheses after quote: (*HL*).

30 Cooper, p.83.

31 Starhawk, *The Spiral Dance: A Rebirth of the Ancient Religion of the Great Goddess* (San Francisco: Harper Collins, 1999), p.3.

32 Nevill Drury, *The Watkins Dictionary of Magic* (London: Watkins, 2005), p.34.

33 *Ibid*, p.295.

34 Dion Fortune, *Psychic Self-Defence* (San Francisco: Red Wheel, 1986), p.190.

35 Christ, p.161.

36 *Ibid.*

37 Dion Fortune, *The Mystical Qabalah* (London: Ernest Benn, 1974), p.29.

38 Bettleheim, p.8.

39 Kate Bush quoted in Whiteley, *Too Much*, p.81.

40 Irigaray, *Sexes*, p.62.

41 Gordon, p.43.

42 As quoted in John Sakamoto, 'Kate Bush weaves a fairy tale,' *Toronto Sun* (14 Dec 1993). Available online: http://gaffa.org/reaching/i93_tsu.html. Last accessed: 13 Oct 2008.

The rebirth of the BFS

1 Papadopolous, Dimitris, Niamh Stephenson, Vassilly Tsianos, *Escape Routes: Control and Subversion in the 21st Century* (London: Pluto 2008).

2 See Moy, p.38-40 and Kruse, p.455.

3 Moy, p.39.

4 Stanislav Grof, *The Ultimate Journey: Consciousness and the Mystery of Death* (Ben Lomand: MAPS, 2006), p.22.

5 Diane Purkiss, *The Witch in History: Early Modern and Twentieth Century Representations* (London: Routledge, 1996), p.9.

6 *Ibid*, p.10.

7 Gauthier, p.201.

8 As quoted in Richard Skinner, 'Classic Albums interview: Hounds Of Love,' *BBC Radio 1* (26 Jan 1985). Available online: http://gaffa.org/reaching/ir85_r1.htm. Last accessed: 13 Oct 2008.

9 Hester, Marianne, *Lewd Women and Wicked Witches: A Study of the Dynamics of Male Domination* (London: Routledge, 1992), p.185.

10 Emily Dickinson, '501,' in Thomas H. Johnson (ed.), *Emily Dickinson: The Complete Poems* (London: Faber, 1975) p.243.

11 Teresa de Lauretis, 'Fem/Les Scramble,' in Dana Heller (ed.), *Cross Purposes: Lesbians, Feminists and the Limits of Alliance* (Bloomington: Indiana University Press, 1997), pp.42-49 (p.43).

12 Anon, 'Jig of Life,' *A Best of' Love-Hounds Collection* (11 Oct 1985). Available online: http://gaffa.org/dreaming/tnw_song.html#jig. Last accessed: 13 Oct 2008. Because these words are not printed on the lyric sheet, interpretations have varied over whether the words refer to 'life' or 'light.' It makes sense to me, in the context of memories and ancient lineages, that 'life' is the word used.

13 Grof, p.32.

14 Kate Bush, *Aerial* (EMI: 0946 3 43960 2 8), 2005. All future references to the album will be included in the body of the text in italicized parentheses as follows (*A*).

15 René Descartes, 'Discourse On The Method Of Rightly Conducting The Reason And Seeking For Truth In The Sciences,' *Key Philosophical Writings*, trans. by Elizabeth S. Haldane and G. R. T. Ross (Hertfordshire: Wordsworth Editions, 1997), pp.71-122 (p.108). Italics mine.

16 Braidotti, *Transpositions*, p.261.

17 Starhawk, *The Earth Path* (San Francisco: Harper Collins, 2004), p.87.

18 Braidotti, *Transpositions*, p.261.

Glossary

ADRIANA CAVARERO : Italian philosopher. She argues we become aware of the unique, singularity of people through hearing their voice. This voice is not spoken in isolation from others, but always in relation to others.

BECOMING : A theory developed by 20th century French philosophers Gilles Deleuze and Felix Guattari. Becoming is a way of understanding how subjects are formed with each other in an encounter between entities (for example, between a human and a tree). Becoming is a way of understanding how life is enriched through being open to encounters with others, as both entities become more than what they were before.

BFS : Stands for the Bushian Feminine Subject. 'Bushian' meaning derived from Kate Bush, 'Feminine' because she creates a space where feminine power can be experienced within popular culture, and 'Subject' refers to subjectivity (see 'Subjectivity'). The BFS is the main character in the story of the book and goes through many changes as she undertakes her journey through Kate Bush's music.

CARTESIAN SUBJECT/ LIBERAL HUMANISM : The model of being developed by René Descartes in the 17th century, in many ways is the foundation for the societies we live in today. Descartes is known for the instigating hierarchical, dualistic ways of understanding the world ('subject/object,' 'mind/body') that place things in opposition to each other. This means that one term is structured as superior to the other ('man/'woman,' 'human'/'animal'). This creates a relationship of negative difference where the positive term has grounds to oppress the negative term because they are positioned as superior to them. The Cartesian subject is the bedrock of liberal humanism, a philosophy that emerged during the Enlightenment. This was a time that privileged rational thinking and placed it at the heart of the political and social order.

DESIRE : An important quality of the BFS. Her desire is autonomous, self-sustaining, and is a vital power generating her life force.

FEMINISM(s) : Social movement and philosophy that has taken on many different forms in its history, and means vastly different things depending on what type of feminist you are. The type of feminism that the BFS embodies celebrates the independent desire of women. She presents feminine sexual difference as a multiplying force drawn from the power of women's bodies. She seeks to carve out an embodied space for women's stories and mythologies to become a permanent part of cultural reality.

FLUIDITY : Another important quality of the BFS, for she is a shape-shifter. She is able to move between categories, identities and realities in a fluid manner. She cannot be pinned down to one place or person and is always prone to change and transformation.

IMMANENCE : The idea that there is a divine presence that exists within, or is inherent to, the material world. It suggests that spirituality is resolutely of 'this world,' rather than being split off, or transcendent to, some heavenly realm we cannot touch with our hands.

JUDITH BUTLER : American philosopher famous for causing gender trouble within feminism in the 1990s with her theory of performativity. Butler argues that there is no essence to gender, and gender only comes to appear as natural in society because it is continually repeated. Using the example of drag, she suggests that these repetitions always miss the mark, allowing us to see the ways gender is constructed, rendering it unstable and changeable. Her later work is concerned with ethics and what counts as a human, or grievable life.

LUCE IRIGARAY : French philosopher who argues that for equality between the sexes to emerge, there needs to be the recognition of female sexual difference. In the 1970s and 1980s she advocated the need to create an alternative female symbolic economy that would draw upon the physical and rhythmical difference of the female sex. Often criticised for presenting essentialist ideas about women, her theories locate sexual difference as a relational difference, rather than as being exclusively tied to the body. Her work is also interested in theories of divinity, and argues that society requires an equality of divine female references and symbols to the male.

MAGICK : A way of shaping unseen forces in order to transform the nature of reality. The deployment of ritual symbols and spells, to achieve desired effect.

MULTIPLICITY : An important quality of the BFS. Theoretically her multiplicity is achieved through her embodiment of feminine sexual difference and through being open transformation with others in the process of becoming. Her multiplicity allows her to change and become many different things throughout her life.

NON HUMAN : A large category that encompasses everything that isn't human – animals, plants, machines.

ONTOLOGY : The theory of being. Society is organised based on presumptions about the nature of being. For example, one idea about being is that men are superior to women, or that humans are superior to animals. Another would be that neither men nor women; humans nor animals are superior, and that these categories (and lived realities) naturally enrich each other. Ontological assumptions have implications on how society is arranged. They effect commonsense (and unconscious) assumptions about how we relate to and with each other.

ORIENTALISM : Concept defined by American Palestinian cultural critic Edward Said. He argued that 'Eastern cultures' have, since the 19th century, been stereotyped by the West as hyper-sexualised, heathen, despotic and uncivilised. This presentation of the East was in contrast to the West, which was presented as civilised and rational. Such racist ideas were used as the cultural justification for colonial enterprises in the 19th century, and still occur within cultural representations today.

POST-HUMAN : A critique of humanist thinking that challenges its anthropocentrism. Anthropocentrism suggests the human is the centre of the universe, and has an exclusive possession of all knowledge. Post-humanism focuses on encounters between the multiple species that live on the earth (including animals and machines). Post-humanism is more interactive than humanist philosophy, since it shows how humans are transformed (and re-arranged) through exposure with their environment.

POST-STRUCTURALISM : Name for a group of diverse philosophical positions that came to prominence in the 1960s onwards. Post-structuralists can be broadly connected by how they focus on language as a site of analysis. They suggest that it is within language where meaning is constructed. This idea posed a radical challenge to humanist thinking which is premised on the idea that the humans created meaning. Another important point about post-structuralism is that it is based on a notion of subjectivity which is decentred, or split. A post-structuralist would say we do not always 'know' what we are doing or why we are doing it. This again is a challenge to the liberal humanist subject who would say 'I think therefore I am.'

QUEER : Activist and theoretical term that developed in the 1980s and 1990s to create a coalitional space for lesbian, gay, bisexual, transgender and intersex people in the face of the AIDS crisis. The play of queer and querying implied a questioning of all kinds of normative behaviour relating to sexuality, gender, race, class and physical ability. Queer theory was an attempt to offer analysis which accounted for how oppressions intersected with each other. Queer was also presented as an anti-identity, since it sought to erode the borders between supposedly stable categories such as man/woman, straight/gay.

REBIRTH : The fundamental quality of the BFS. Rebirth enables her to create new identities within her life. Her ability to be reborn underlines her resilience and capacity to survive death.

SUBJECTIVITY : A concept developed in post-structuralist theory that explores how, as individuals, we both have control over our lives (we are the subjects), and we are subjected to forces that are outside of our control (such as gender, class, race, the opinions of others). Subjectivity can be understood simultaneously as a site of struggle *and* transformation.

SYMBOLS : The concentration of an idea within an object or person used to create meaning. Repeating a symbol serves to bind its power further, as they become familiar and recognised within the cultural imaginaries.

Bibliography

Andersen, Hans Christian, 'The Red Shoes,' in Hans Christian Andersen, *The Complete Fairy Tales* (Ware: Wordsworth, 1998), pp.322-329.

Anon, 'The Story of Lucy Wan,' in A.L. Lloyd and R. Vaughan Williams (eds.), *The Penguin Book of English Folk Songs* (London: Penguin, 1961), p.65.

Anon, '*Lionheart* Promo Cassette,' *EMI* Canada (1978).
Available online: http://gaffa.org/reaching/im78_lh.html. Last accessed 13 Oct 2008.

Anon, 'KB On Tour,' *Nationwide* TV Programme (4 Apr 1979).
Available online: http://gaffa.org/reaching/iv79_ot.html. Last accessed 13 Oct 2008.

Anon, 'Unknown BBC interview,' *BBC* (1982).
Available online: http://gaffa.org/cloud/music/the_dreaming.html. Last accessed 13 Oct 2008.

Anon, 'Jig of Life,' *A Best of Love-Hounds Collection* (11 Oct 1985).
Available online: http://gaffa.org/dreaming/tnw_song.html#jig. Last accessed 13 Oct 2008.

Barad, Karen, *Meeting the Universe Halfway: Quantum Physics and the Entanglement of Matter and Meaning* (Durham: Duke University Press, 2007).

Barrie, JM, *Peter Pan in Kensington Gardens / Peter and Wendy* (Oxford: Oxford World's Classics, 1999).

Bersani, Leo, *Homos* (Cambridge: Harvard University Press, 1995).

Bettleheim, Bruno, *The Uses of Enchantment: The Meaning and Importance of Fairy Tales* (London: Penguin, 1991).

Bhabha, Homi, *The Location of Culture* (London: Routledge, 1994).

Blackman, Lisa et al, 'Creating Subjectivities,' in *Subjectivity* (2008) 22: 1-27.

Boone, Joseph, 'Vacation Cruises; or, The Homoerotics of Orientalism,' in John Hawley (ed.), *Post-Colonial, Queer* (New York: SUNY, 2001), pp. 43-78.

Boulous Walker, Michelle, *Philosophy and the Maternal Body: Reading Silence* (London: Routledge, 1999).

Braidotti, Rosi, *Transpositions: On Sustainable Nomadic Ethics* (Cambridge: Polity Press, 2006).

Brontë, Charlotte, *Jane Eyre* (London: Penguin, 2006).

Bush, Kate, 'Self Portrait,' *The Kick Inside* promo LP/cassette Interview (1978). Available online: http://gaffa.org/reaching/im78_tki.html. Last accessed 13 Oct 2008.

Bush, Kate, 'Hello Everybody,' *KBC 2* (Summer 1979). Available online: http://gaffa.org/garden/kate2.html. Last accessed 13 Oct 2008.

Bush, Kate, 'Kate's KBC article,' *KBC 3* (Nov 1979). Available online: http://gaffa.org/garden/kate3.html. Last accessed 13 Oct 2008.

Bush, Kate, 'Kate's KBC article,' *KBC 12* (Oct 1982). Available online: http://gaffa.org/garden/kate14.html. Last accessed 14 Oct 2008.

Bush, Kate, 'Kate Bush's KBC article,' *KBC 16* (n.d) Available online: http://gaffa.org/garden/kate18.html. Last accessed 13 Oct 2008.

Butler, Judith, *Frames of War: When is Life Grievable?* (London: Verso, 2009).

Butler, Judith, *Gender Trouble: Feminism and the Subversion of Identity* (London: Routledge, 1993).

Campbell, Joseph, *Hero With a Thousand Faces* (Princeton: Princeton University Press, 1968).

Carter, Angela (ed.), *The Virago Book of Fairy Tales* (London: Virago, 1991).

Cavarero, Adriana, *For More Than One Voice: Towards a Philosophy of Vocal Expression* (Stanford: Stanford University Press, 2005).

Charles, Hugh and Ross Parker, 'There'll always be an England,' *Sterling Times: The Virtual Scrapbook of British Nostalgia*. Available online: http://sterlingtimes.co.uk/alwaysengland.html. Last accessed 13 Oct 2008.

Chopin, Kate, *The Awakening and Selected Stories* (London: Penguin, 2003).

Christ, Carol P. and Judith Plaskow (eds.), *Womanspirit Rising: A Feminist Reader in Religion* (San Francisco: Harper Collins, 1992).

Christ, Carol P., *Rebirth of the Goddess: Finding Meaning in Feminist Spirituality* (London: Routledge, 2004).

Cixous, Hélène, 'The Laugh of the Medusa,' in Robyn R. Warhol and Diane Price Herndl (eds.), *Feminisms: An Anthology of Literary Theory and Criticism* (Basingstoke: Macmillan, 1997), pp.335-342.

Cixous, Hélène, 'Sorties Out and Out: Attacks/Ways Out/Forays,' in Hélène Cixous and Catherine Clemènt, *The Newly Born Woman*, trans. Betsy Wing (Manchester: Manchester University Press, 1993), pp.63-134.

Cook, Richard, 'My music sophisticated? I'd rather you said that than turdlike!' *New Musical Express* (Oct 1992).
Available online: http://gaffa.org/cloud/music/leave_it_open.html. Last accessed 13 Oct 2008.

Cooper, J.C., *Symbolic and Mythological Animals* (London: Harper Collins, 1992).

Copeland, Roger, 'Dance, Feminism and the Critique of the Visual,' in Helen Thomas (ed.), *Dance, Gender and Culture* (Basingstoke: Macmillan, 1993), pp.134-145.

Cvetkovich, Ann, *An Archive of Feelings: Trauma, Sexuality and Lesbian Public Cultures* (Durham: Duke University Press, 2003).

de Lauretis, Teresa, 'Fem/Les Scramble', in Dana Heller (ed.), *Cross Purposes: Lesbians, Feminists and the Limits of Alliance* (Bloomington: Indiana University Press, 1997), pp.42-49.

Deleuze, Gilles and Felix Guattari, *A Thousand Plateaus*, trans. Brian Massumi (London: Continuum, 2004).

Descartes, René, 'Discourse On the Method Of Rightly Conducting The Reason And Seeking For Truth In The Sciences,' *Key Philosophical Writings*, trans. Elizabeth S. Haldane and G. R. T. Ross (Hertfordshire: Wordsworth Editions, 1997), pp.71-122.

Dickinson, Emily, '501', in Thomas H. Johnson (ed.), *Emily Dickinson: The Complete Poems* (London: Faber, 1975) p.243.

Dickinson, Emily, '1383', in Thomas H. Johnson (ed.), *Emily Dickinson: The Complete Poems* (London: Faber, 1975), p 594.

Doherty, Harry, 'The Kick Outside,' *Melody Maker* (3 June 1978).
Available online: http://gaffa.org/reaching/i78_mm2.html. Last accessed 12 Oct 2008.

Drury, Nevill, *The Watkins Dictionary of Magic* (London: Watkins, 2005).

Dyer, Richard, *The Culture of Queers* (London: Routledge, 2002).

Fitzgerald-Morris, Krystyna Peter Fitzgerald-Morris and David Cross (eds.), *HomeGround: The Kate Bush Magazine* (1982 – now).
Available online: http://katebushnews.com/homegrou.htm. Last accessed 18 Oct 2008.

Fortune, Dion, *Psychic Self-Defence* (San Francisco: Red Wheel, 1986).

Fortune, Dion, *The Mystical Qabbalah* (London: Ernest Benn, 1974).

Gauthier, Xavière, 'Why Witches?' in Elaine Marks and Isabelle de Courtivron (eds.), *New French Feminisms: An Anthology* (New York: Harvester, 1981), pp.199-203.

Gordon, Bonnie, 'Kate Bush's Subversive Shoes,' *Women and Music: A Journal of Gender and Culture* 9 (2005), pp.37-50.

Grof, Stanislav, *The Ultimate Journey: Consciousness and the Mystery of Death* (Ben Lomand: MAPS, 2006).

Grosz, Elizabeth, *Volatile Bodies: Towards a Corporeal Feminism* (Bloomington: Indiana University Press, 1994).

Guiley, Rosemary Ellen, 'Witchcraft as Goddess Worship,' in Carolyne Addington (ed.), *The Feminist Companion to Mythology* (London: Pandora, 1992), pp.418-425.

Halberstam, Judith, *In a Queer Time and Place: Transgender Bodies, Subcultural Lives* (New York: New York University Press, 2005).

Halberstam, Judith, *Female Masculinity* (Durham: Duke University Press, 1998).

Haraway, Donna, *Modest_Witness@Second Millenium FemaleMan-Meets-Oncomouse: Feminism and Technoscience* (London: Routledge, 1997).

Haraway, Donna, *Simians, Cyborgs and Women: The Reinvention of Nature* (London: Free Association Books, 1991).

Hester, Marianne, *Lewd Women and Wicked Witches: A Study of the Dynamics of Male Domination* (London: Routledge, 1992).

Hume, Lynne, 'The Dreaming in Contemporary Aboriginal Australia,' in Graham Harvey (ed.), *Indigenous Religions: A Companion* (London: Cassell, 2000), pp.124-136.

Irigaray, Luce, 'Introduction: Spirituality and Religion,' in Luce Irigaray (ed.), *Key Writings* (London: Continuum, 2004), pp.145-150.

Irigaray, Luce, *This Sex Which is Not One*, trans. Catherine Porter, (Ithaca: Cornell University Press, 1985).

Irigaray, Luce, 'How Can We Live Together in a Lasting way?' in Luce Irigaray (ed.), *Key Writings* (London: Continuum, 2004), pp.123-133.

Irigaray, Luce, 'The Age of the Breath,' in, Luce Irigaray (ed.), *Key Writings* (London: Continuum, 2004), pp.165-170.

Irigaray, Luce, 'When our lips speak together,' in Janet Price and Margrit Shildrick (eds.), *Feminist Theory and the Body: A Reader* (Edinburgh: Edinburgh University Press, 1999), pp.82-91.

Irigaray, Luce, *Sexes and Genealogies*, trans. Gillian C. Gill (New York: Columbia University Press, 1982).

Jones, Erica, 'How Kate Bush has inspired a Gay Cult,' *The Pink Paper* (Sep 2005), pp.26-27.

Jovanovich, Rob, *Kate Bush: The Biography* (London: Portrait, 2006).

Kruse, Holly 'In Praise of Kate Bush,' in Simon Frith and Peter Goodwin (eds.), *On Record: Rock, Pop and the Written Word* (London: Routledge, 1990), pp.450-465.

Labelle, Brandon, *Background Noise: A History of Sound Art* (London: Continuum, 2006).

Lehner, Ernst and Joanna Lehner, *Folklore and Symbolism of Flowers, Plants and Trees* (London: Dover Publications, 2004).

Losseff, Nicky, 'Cathy's Homecoming and the Other World: Kate Bush's "Wuthering Heights,"' *Popular Music 18*, (1999) pp. 227-240.

Lukas, Karli, 'Dancing with the Devil You Know: On Powell and Pressburger's *The Red Shoes*,' *Senses of Cinema* (July 2005).
Available online: http://www.sensesofcinema.com/contents/cteq/05/36/red_shoes.html. Last accessed 13 Oct 2006.

Lydon, John quoted on *Queens of British Pop*, BBC One, April 2009.
Available online http://www.bbc.co.uk/musictv/queensofbritishpop/artists/katebush/4/?4. Last accessed 27 Nov 09.

Macfie, A.L., 'Introduction,' in A.L. Macfie (ed.), *Orientalism: A Reader* (Edinburgh: Edinburgh University Press, 2000), pp.2-17.

Mayhew, Emma, 'Positioning the Producer: Gender Divides in Creative Labour and Value,' in Andrew Bennett, Stan Hawkins and Sheila Whiteley (eds.), *Music, Space and Place: Popular Music and Cultural Identity* (Aldershot: Ashgate, 2004), pp.147-154.

McClary, Susan, *Feminine Endings*, (Minnesota: University of Minnesota Press, 1991).

Mitchell, Allyson, 'Deep Lez I Statement.'
Available online http://allysonmitchell.com/action/deeplez.cfm. Last accessed 30 Nov 2009.

Moy, Ron, *Kate Bush and Hounds of Love* (Aldershot: Ashgate, 2007).

Moy, Ron, 'A Daughter of Albion? Kate Bush and mythologies of Englishness,' *Popular Musicology Online* (2006).
Available online: http://www.popular-musicology-online.com/issues/02/moy-01.html. Last accessed 15 Oct 2007.

Mercer, Bob quoted on *Queens of British Pop*, BBC One, April, 2009.
Available online http://bbc.co.uk/musictv/queensofbritishpop/. Last accessed 27 Nov 09.

Mulvey Roberts, Marie, 'Menstrual Misogyny and Taboo: The Medusa, Vampire and Female Stigmatic,' in Andrew Shail and Gillian Howie (eds.), *Menstruation: A Cultural History* (Basingstoke: Palgrave, 2005), pp.149-161.

Negus, Keith, 'Sinead O'Connor – Musical Mother,' in Sheila Whiteley (ed.), *Sexing the Groove: Popular Music and Gender* (London: Routledge, 1997), pp.180-195.

Papadopolous, Dimitris, Niamh Stephenson, Vassilly Tsianos, *Escape Routes: Control and Subversion in the 21st Century* (London: Pluto, 2008).

Purkiss, Diane, *The Witch in History: Early Modern and Twentieth Century Representations* (London: Routledge, 1996).

Radcliffe, Mark 'The Smouldering Gypsy Lover We Would Never Have,' in *The Word*, February 09, Issue 72.

Reilly, Peter, 'Uncaged Bird,' review of *The Kick Inside*, *Stereo* (1978).
Available: http://gaffa.org/reaching/rev_tki.html#stereoreview. Last accessed 27 Feb 2007.

Reynolds, Simon, *Rip It Up and Start Again: Post Punk 1978-1984* (London: Faber, 2005).

Rich, Adrienne, *Compulsory Heterosexuality and Lesbian Existence* (London: Only Women Press, 1981).

Rodger, Gillian, 'Drag, Camp and Gender Subversion in the music and video of Annie Lennox,' *Popular Music* 23: 1 (2004), pp.17-29.

Roseneil, Sasha, *Disarming Patriarchy: Feminism and Political Action at Greenham* (Buckingham: Open University Press, 1995).

Rossetti, Christina, 'The Goblin Market' in *Christina Rossetti, The Complete Poems* (London: Penguin, 2001), pp.5-20.

Rubin, Gayle, 'The Traffic in Women,' in Linda Nicholson (ed.), *Second Wave Feminism: A Reader* (London: Routledge, 1997), pp.28-67.

Sabin, Roger, '"I won't let that dago by": Rethinking Punk and Racism,' in Roger Sabin (ed.), *Punk Rock, So What?: The Cultural Legacy of Punk* (London: Routledge, 1999), pp.199-219.

Sakamoto, John, 'Kate Bush weaves a fairy tale,' *Toronto Sun* (14 Dec1993).
Available online: http://gaffa.org/reaching/i93_tsu.html. Last accessed 13 Oct 2008.

Schaar, Simon, 'Orientalism at the Service of Imperialism,' in A.L. Macfie (ed.), *Orientalism: A Reader* (Edinburgh: Edinburgh University Press, 2000), pp.181-193.

Scott, Derek B., *From the Erotic to the Demonic* (Oxford: Oxford University Press, 2003).

Sexton, Anne, 'The Red Shoes,' in Anne Sexton, *Selected Poems of Anne Sexton* (London: Virago, 1993), p.87.

Shuttle, Penelope and Peter Redgrove, *The Wise Wound: Menstruation and Everywoman* (London: Paladin, 1986).

Showalter, Elaine, *The Female Malady: Women, Madness and English Culture, 1830-1980* (London: Virago, 1987).

Skinner, Richard, 'Classic Albums interview: *Hounds of Love*.' *BBC Radio 1* (26 Jan 1985).
Available online: http://gaffa.org/reaching/ir85_rl.htm. Last accessed 13 Oct 2008.

Spender, Dale, *Man-Made Language* (London: Pandora, 1980).

Spivak, Gayatri Chakravorty, 'Can the Subaltern Speak?' in Cary Nelson and Larry Grossberg (eds.), *Marxism and the Interpretation of Culture* (Urbana, Illinois: University of Illinois Press, 1988), pp.271-313.

Starhawk, *The Earth Path* (San Francisco: Harper Collins, 2004).

Starhawk, *The Spiral Dance: A Rebirth of the Ancient Religion of the Great Goddess* (San Francisco: Harper Collins, 1999).

Stewart, Ed and Sue Cook, 'Personal Call,' *BBC Radio 1* interview (1979). Available online: http://gaffa.org/reaching/ir79_pc.html. Last accessed 13 Oct 2008.

Tatar, Maria, *Off With Their Heads: Fairy Tales and the Culture of Childhood* (Princeton: Princeton University Press, 1992).

Vermorel, Fred, *Secret History of Kate Bush: And the Strange Art of Pop* (London: Omnibus Press, 1983).

Vroomen, Laura, *This Woman's Work: Kate Bush Fans and Practices of Distinction* (Unpublished PhD thesis, Warwick, 2003).

Whiteley, Sheila, 'Kate Bush: The Red Shoes,' *Too Much, Too Young: Popular Music, Age and Gender* (London: Routledge, 2005) pp.70-84

Whiteley, Sheila, *Popular Music and Feminine Sexuality, Identity and Subjectivity* (London, Routledge, 2000).

Wigg, David, 'Wuthering Wonderful,' *Daily Express* (8 Mar 1978). Available online: http://gaffa.org/reaching/i78_de.html. Last accessed 13 Oct 2008.

Wood, Elizabeth, 'Sapphonics,' in Philip Brett, Elizabeth Wood and Gary C. Thomas (eds.), *Queering the Pitch: The New Gay and Lesbian Musicology* (London: Routledge, 1994), pp.27-66.

Music

The Au Pairs, *Sense and Sensuality* (B00005V330). 1982, 2002.

Bush, Kate, *Aerial* (EMI: 0946 3 43960 2 8), 2005.

Bush, Kate, *The Red Shoes* (EMI: B000024BBU), 1993.

Bush, Kate, *The Sensual World* (EMI: B000025VKG), 1989.

Bush, Kate, *Hounds of Love* (EMI: EJ 24 03841), 1985.

Bush, Kate, *The Dreaming* (EMI: EMC 3419 OC 062 64 589), 1982.

Bush, Kate, *Never For Ever* (EMI: 1A 062 07339), 1980.

Bush, Kate, *The Kick Inside* (EMI: EMC 3223 OC 062 06 603), 1978.

Bush, Kate, *Lionheart* (EMI: EMA 787 OC 064 06 859), 1978.

X-Ray Spex, *Germ Free Adolescents* (Sanctuary: B001GU2EC0), 1978.

Film

Bush, Kate, *The Line, The Cross and the Curve* (PMI: MVN 4911853), 1993.

Clayton, Jack, *The Innocents* (20th Century Fox: 6303957064), 1961.

Powell, Michael and Emeric Pressburger, *The Red Shoes* (Carlton: VFB22329), 1948, 2001.

printed and bound by Lightning Source UK

Lightning Source UK Ltd.
Milton Keynes UK
UKHW01f0848260918
329556UK00001B/68/P